For my parents,
Marvin and Gwen Cowart,
who showed me how to battle
long before I ever had to
fight on my own.

And to the eleven men
in my Battle Small Group
at New Covenant Church
who helped make this
book a reality.

TABLE OF CONTENTS

FOR YOURSELF YOUR MARRIAGE YOUR FAMILY

BATTLE

JASON JOHN COWART

WHY THE BATTLE

The very first thing to mention might be the reason for this book and study. We all face battles, but this book and study was born out of a very specific issue in the life of my family.

Around 2015 or so, my wife and oldest daughter, and several in my wife's side of the family were diagnosed with a genetic disorder called CTLA-4. Basically what this disorder does is that it causes auto immune issues. CTLA-4 is a protein receptor that functions as an immune checkpoint and down-regulates immune responses. Essentially, when your body gets an infection, your immune system goes to battle against the infection, however, with CTLA-4, your body not only fights the infection, but it begins to fight against your organs as well because the protein that is supposed to tell your immune system to stop is not present. With my wife and daughter, the symptoms are minimal, however, in my wife's family, there are a variety of serious medical issues. In fact, the way this was all discovered was based on my brother-in-law nearly dying from brain lesions as a result of the CTLA-4 mutation. The Veteran's Affairs hospital in Houston did a biopsy on these lesions and a random tech, on a whim, happened to send a sample to the National Institute of Health (NIH) for research. When they got the biopsy, amazingly, there was a specific doctor involved in a study on this very disorder. With only like 50 people in the US having this issue, it was a pretty incredible thing and a huge blessing, as the treatments that resulted not only saved his life, but has made the quality of life for those in our extended family with symptoms from the disorder exponentially better. The NIH has really been a godsend to us, and we are monumentally thankful to God and the doctors working hard for a cure.

My wife and daughter are a part of this research study and have to go to the NIH every year to remain in the study. In 2019, they went for their normal testing and my daughter failed a basic glucose test. They decided to keep her an extra day to do a three hour test. Unfortunately, she failed that test as well by the slimmest of margins. So they essentially diagnosed her with the early stages of type 1 diabetes. While this is not a death sentence, it is very troubling. Any parent wants their child to be in perfect health, and would gladly trade their good health for their kid's genetic disorder. I was no different. The news was very difficult for me to take in.

Several years before this all happened, and right about the time the CTLA-4 issue was discovered, my wife went to Pink Impact at Gateway Church in Southlake, Texas. During the conference, Jimmy Evans spoke, and as he often does, he took time at the end to speak prophetically. In that moment he said, "Someone here has recently found out that you have a genetic disorder. God wants you to know that he sees the issue and that he is still in control. You need not fear. God will give you a new bloodline. And your greatest fear, that it will impact your children, will be put to rest. You have a new bloodline." In a sea of 4000+ women, he could have only been more specific had he said her name. While that is amazing, what is more astonishing is that years later, the day that my daughter had the glucose test, the one she was kept a day longer than she was scheduled, my wife woke up and checked her Facebook and the memory on that specific day was the video she recorded at Pink Impact when Jimmy Evans gave that prophetic word. So obviously God was trying to do something there. The news was so difficult for me, but God was clearly reminding us to trust him.

They returned home on a Friday, and late that night, around midnight, I was getting cleaned up to go to bed. I got in the shower and instantly felt this intense urge, this burden, that I had to pray right then. It wasn't a little, cute, "God, I hope everything works out" kind of prayer. It was militant. It was aggressive. It was a battle. It was, "Satan, how dare you? How dare you attack my family? How dare you rear your head? How dare you go against the promise of God he has given to us? Jesus took stripes on his back for my wife and daughter's healing. They have said yes to Jesus. They are bought with his blood. What are you thinking right now?" It was angry and strong. I prayed until the water went cold, half in English and half in the Spirit. I prayed long enough to turn into a prune. But as I began to wind down, I felt this peace come over me like I have rarely felt before. I heard the Lord say to me, "Expect results. Expect results. Expect results. I don't care what the charts say. I am not concerned with what the doctors say. Trust me and expect results." He kept saying it over and over again. I took that as a breakthrough for me personally that I needed to stand on God's Word, on his promise, and not be afraid. I had entered into an all-out attack, a war, and I needed to battle for my family.

A few weeks later they came back from a series of treatments that had actually reversed a diabetes diagnosis in one other CTLA-4 patient, and while it seemed my daughter's anti-insulin antibodies were going in the right direction, the doctor mentioned trying a more aggressive, less safe, experimental drug, as the current treatment regimen was either not working, or else the disease was progressing faster than they thought. So there I was, having to decide whether or not I was going to trust God's Word or not. Was I going to expect results, or was I going to let fear run amok in my family?

This is why this book exists. I had to remember in that moment what my parents taught me long ago. My dad is not a "back down from a battle" kind of guy. My mother is not a "lay down and get run over" type of woman. They taught me a long time ago that sometimes you have to stand up and fight. Of course, not every day is a battle, and you aren't charging

3

the front lines every second, but there are moments in your life when you need to get to fighting because the war is raging and you have to either engage or be crushed. I was desperate, not only to remind myself how to fight like I had been taught, but to help others, especially men, learn how to fight the enemy, to get some understanding of this.

Consider what the Bible tells us in Ephesians 6:12

> "For we do not wrestle against flesh and blood, but against the rulers, against the authorities, against the cosmic powers over this present darkness, against the spiritual forces of evil in the heaven-ly places."

We fight on three fronts that we see in this verse. The first one is spiritual. There is always a spiritual fight, but realisze we may not always have to be engaged in battle in that moment, much like soldiers in a war. Some are at the barracks while others are on missions. But while there is not always a battle before you, we are in a constant war. The spiritual is always where the fight originates. I have had to learn that what is going on in the natural is really just a reflection of what is going on in the spiritual. The spiritual fight is always, however, the fight that matters. We are spiritual beings with a physical body, not the other way around. I have to remind myself of this constantly, because the first front is always spiritual.

The second is physical. While we may not wrestle against flesh and blood, as the verse says, the enemy is very quick to attack us physically. He will attack your family, your kids, and he won't care how low the blow is. The very week I spoke for the first time at New Covenant Church in 2014 where I was an associate pastor, my son, my two-month-old at the time, stopped breathing. My wife performed CPR and he was rushed to the ER. There I was at one in the morning waiting while my baby boy was getting a spinal tap. That will distract you, for sure. That is how dirty the enemy plays. There are no rules with him. There is no Geneva Conven-tion with Satan. He is dirty and he will play that way. Perhaps it was a co-

4

ncidence, but I don't believe that for a second. I have had to engage the enemy too many times to believe in coincidental attacks. It was intentional and abhorrent in that he used my baby son to fight me. But that is who Satan is, so you have to go into this battle knowing that he is like that. It is a spiritual war, but you need to know that at any point, he will try to attack you and your family physically. You have to stay vigilant. The physical battle is almost always pointing to the reality in the spiritual, and while it is important not to live life thinking there's a devil behind every little thing that happens in the natural, it is important that you remember that you are a spirit with a body and he will attack your body to wound your spirit.

The last one is the soul, which I call your mind, will, and emotions. Most people live driven by their soul, which directs the physical, and with little to no thought about the spiritual. You should always be driven by the Spirit, which directs the soul, and finally, the physical. When you are led by your fleshly mind, will, emotions, you are not battling the Ephesians 6:12 war. You

> **REMEMBER THAT YOU ARE A SPIRIT WITH A BODY AND SATAN WILL ATTACK YOUR BODY TO WOUND YOUR SPIRIT.**

have to keep that in the forefront of your mind. It is easy to get angry and frustrated, and it isn't always about your kid having a sickness or something like I was dealing with. It is when you and your wife have been trying to get on the same page in your communication, and she gives you one cross look, and all of the sudden, you erupt in that moment. That is a spiritual battle, not a physical one. It isn't her. It is the enemy. You have to learn how to control your mind, will, and emotions. In the next chapter, we will talk about how to control yourself as a soldier because if you don't take care of your own life and relationship with Jesus and have that all in the right context, then you are going to be worthless in the battle. No one wants to go to battle next to a 452 pound lazy soldier that has become careless and lax. We all want Rambo next to us. We all want a spiritual Arnold Schwarzenegger going to battle with us, and what that means is that there are going to be times when I need to rely on the people around me who are in the battle with me. I need my brothers at arms in the right place, fit for the battle. That means I need to be as well, and in this soul realm is where he loves to attack. There's no place Satan attacks us more than in this area of our soul, our mind, will, and emotions.

In light of these battle fronts, there are typically two ways we respond to the attack. Fear is the primary human emotion. Our fleshly response to negative stimuli is fear, and has been since the garden. Did you know that "Do not fear/be afraid" is mentioned around 365 times in the Bible. Obviously, God knew that fear would be a struggle for us. Consider what Philippians 4:6-7 says,

> "...do not be anxious about anything, but in everything by prayer and supplication with thanksgiving let your requests be made known to God. And the peace of God, which surpasses all under-standing, will guard your hearts and your minds in Christ Jesus."

Our natural reaction to a battle is fear, but our natural reaction should be to press into God. We can see this in Genesis 3:10.

> "And he (Adam) said, 'I heard the sound of you in the garden, and I was afraid, because I was naked, and I hid myself.'"

This is Adam talking to God, the one who literally spoke the universe into existence. "I was afraid so I hid myself." One would think that what happens when the battle comes to us and the pressure is on, since our human nature is to respond in fear, that we would simply be paralyzed with fear in that moment, but it is quite the contrary, actually. Fear tends to make us run. It is the fight or flight mechanism. Many times we run away from God, specifically, but we always run to something specific. I have found that more times than not, that fear makes us run to the thing we see as our source. This is a huge problem because if your source isn't God, then you are going to be feeding the fire of the battle with gasoline of fear. Money is not your source. There isn't enough money to make my kid's mmune system work right and stop diabetes in her. What about pride? If you are such a big, strong, buff guy, and so full of pride about your ability to protect and provide for your family that you can't break down in front of another brother and say, "Listen man, I am struggling and I need your help," then what you've done is that you've made yourself your source, and all this battle is going to do is to feed the fear that got you into what you think is your source in the first place. You have to respond in a different way. Previously in the Garden, there was close communication and no need for fear. After the fall, there was fear that hindered the communication between God and man. The result was a breakdown not only in the relationship, but in the family. We see this in the fact that the entire family, and the entirety of humanity, began acting out of fear. While fear is our natural human response to a battle, we must remember that as Spirit-filled children of God, we are not driven by our flesh.

Many times in my own life, I find I respond out of fear and in my flesh rather than what I should respond in. For me personally, I tend to respond in frustration and anger. When I get fleshly, I will get frustrated at a situation rather than being calm and getting my mind right. When that happens, I can't even remember 20 minutes later what I was frustrated about! But what it is in me is the same in all of us. It is this autonomic response to negative stimuli that we have to change. How do we change that? We have to change how we respond.

We have to respond in faith. Hebrews 11:1 gives us the definition of faith.

> "Now faith is the assurance of things hoped for, the conviction of things not seen."

Faith is the bridge that gets us from the place where logic ends to the place where an experience with Jesus begins. Think about that for a moment because when you are looking at a situation, facing the battle, whether in the spiritual or natural, there is going to be a moment where your logic just doesn't work anymore. You are going to say, "Wait, I can't figure this out." This is the point where logic fails. But what God wants you to do in the midst of this battle, is to jump from logic into an experience with Jesus. God will often allow battles in our lives just for the purpose of getting us to this point! While we would love to just jump from logic to experience, there is something that has to bridge the divide, something that gets you from logic to experience. That is faith. The purpose of faith is to bridge the gap between logic and experience. What I was having to walk through in terms of my wife and daughter and their medical issue, there was no logical explanation why we were having to go through that. Out of 400 million Americans, why were some of the people I love the most on earth included in that 50? It defies logic. God had already told me what he was going to do. He said we would experience a new bloodline. Well, we weren't seeing that, and let's be honest, it isn't logical for their blood to change within their own bodies miraculously anyway. But if we were going to get from bad blood to new blood, that experiential moment with Jesus where we saw them healed, it was going to take faith. We had to step into faith until the experience happened. It is hard walking in faith. You never see the whole path, and often you can't see the next step. That is why the Bible tells us that we walk by faith and not by sight. You have to trust God that when he promises that he orders our steps, he means it. When he promises that we will not dash our feet against a stone, it means that he already knows the places where he wants our feet to fall. My job in that moment is not to try to be the bridge between logic and experience, but simply to have faith that God can be trusted and that he will accomplish what he promised. So we need to be sure we are responding out of faith, not fear. Faith is believing not only that the fight is not physical, but that we are uniquely advantaged and already victorious because of Jesus. 1 Samuel 17:47 promises us,

> **FAITH IS THE BRIDGE THAT GETS US FROM THE PLACE WHERE LOGIC ENDS TO THE PLACE WHERE AN EXPERIENCE WITH JESUS BEGINS.**

"The battle is the Lord's."

Many times we go into the battle thinking it is all on us and that we have to make the victory happen in our own strength, after all, we are the men of the house and our family is looking to us. That isn't the truth at all. Now, you do have a responsibility, which we'll talk about next chapter, but at the end of the day, your job is to trust God and operate out of faith knowing that God is going to take care of the situation - whether he does what you expect him to do or not. Faith is what gets you to the second part of Philippians 4:6-7,

> "And the peace of God, which surpasses all understanding, will guard your hearts and your minds in Christ Jesus."

The opposite of fear is not courage, it is peace. Fear creates torment, and faith through love creates peace in our hearts. Now we see in 1 John 4:18,

> "Perfect love casts out fear."

It isn't a contradiction to say that the opposite of fear is peace and not love, because you mind would think, "If love casts out fear, then love must be the opposite of fear," and perhaps an argument can be made about that. But I think that it is not a contradiction between love and peace, but rather, it is a completion of those two. Love removes fear so that peace can reign in our hearts. We have to respond by faith.

Let me stop at this moment and just ask you to reflect on your own life. How are you responding to your battles?

This is an important question because your reactions are always monumentally more important than the action. I had a pastor once tell me, "It is never the action, it is always your reaction that matters most." So we have to think about how we react to the attack because our response is always more powerful than the attack. Why is this the case? It is because your response lets the enemy know exactly what he has done to you, what is working against you. If sexual immorality is a struggle and some beautiful woman with a short skirt walks in and it catches your attention, the enemy sees your response, and I guarantee, when you are home alone later on, or even laying there next to your wife in bed trying to go to sleep, the enemy will attack you with that experience. He is going to find your weak spot and he will exploit it. Many times he finds the weak spots in our lives, the kinks in our armor, based on how we respond to his attack. When a doctor is giving you a physical exam and he touches one knee and you don't respond, but then he touches the other one and you grimace in pain, then your response has told the doctor that there is a problem here - in spite of what your mouth might say! The same thing happens spiritually. How you respond is really going to be a key in how you battle.

I was thinking about opposing responses to an attack that we see in the text of the Bible, and none could be better than two we see in the episode of David and Goliath. The first is Saul's response in 1 Samuel 17:11.

> "When Saul and all Israel heard these words of the Philistine, they were dismayed and greatly afraid."

Saul's fear kept him in the tent when he should have been on the front lines. He almost lost the entire country. I guarantee you that if at any moment the Philistine army would have attacked Israel, they would have fallen. Too many times, we see men, even men that we perceive as strong, godly men, sitting in their tents while their family is being ravaged by the enemy. Honestly, I am tired of seeing that. I am tired of men taking inferior roles in the leading of their family. I am tired of seeing men not stepping up to be the leaders of their house. That doesn't mean being dictatorial, where you demand and command. Not at all. Remember, as husbands, we are supposed to love our wives like Christ loves the church and gave himself for her. It isn't about being a tyrant, it is about stepping up and taking on the mantle of your role. Saul should have been doing what David

10

was doing. So what was David doing?

In 1 Samuel 17:19-26, we see David's response.

> "Now Saul and they and all the men of Israel were in the Valley
> of Elah, fighting with the Philistines. And David rose early in the
> morning and left the sheep with a keeper and took the provisions
> and went, as Jesse had commanded him. And he came to the
> encampment as the host was going out to the battle line, shouting
> the war cry. And Israel and the Philistines drew up for battle, army
> against army. And David left the things in charge of the keeper of
> the baggage and ran to the ranks and went and greeted his broth-
> ers. As he talked with them, behold, the champion, the Philistine of
> Gath, Goliath by name, came up out of the ranks of the Philistines
> and spoke the same words as before. And David heard him. All
> the men of Israel, when they saw the man, fled from him and were
> much afraid. And the men of Israel said, 'Have you seen this man
> who has come up? Surely he has come up to defy Israel. And the
> king will enrich the man who kills him with great riches and will
> give him his daughter and make his father's house free in Israel.'
> And David said to the men who stood by him, 'What shall be done
> for the man who kills this Philistine and takes away the reproach
> from Israel? For who is this uncircumcised Philistine, that he
> should defy the armies of the living God?'"

Let me ask you this. When is the last time you stood up in the face of the
enemy and said, "Who do you think you are coming in to try to defy the
living God, to try to take my family? Who do you think you are? What are
your thinking? To come into my home with this mess?" We have got to
learn how to be militant against the enemy. It is not wrong to burn with
righteous anger against the enemy. That is exactly what I did that night
my family came home from the NIH. It was a righteous and holy anger at
an enemy trying to devour my family, to steal, and I wasn't going to let it
happen. I refused to back down. I stood up to fight, to fight until I had no

fight left within me, to fight until Satan ripped the sword of the Spirit from my cold, dead fingers before I let him take my kid away from me. We've got to get that inside of us. This is a fight! The devil is not going to relent or back down. We have to fight. We have to respond, and that response is literally everything!

We have to respond in these three ways, and the first is prayer. Prayer does two things: it focuses our attention on God, and it gives us time to respond well. I don't know about you, but I tend to respond out of a gut reaction, and five times out of ten, it isn't the right one. It is a great way to get your arm cut off in the middle of the battle. But here's the thing we have to think about: there is no battle that is on you so quick that you can't take a moment and pray, not a single one.

When my son stopped breathing and we had to rush him to the hospital, I was at Walmart at the moment all of this went down. My wife called, frantic, telling me he wasn't breathing. I told her to do CPR and call 911, and that I was coming home. A funny part of this story was that I had played church league softball that night and had a giant strawberry on my leg from sliding on the so-called dirt infield. More like concrete! Because it hurt so bad, I asked the lady at the entrance to Walmart for one of those electric carts. She gave me that look that said, "Hmm, I don't know about this." I assured her I wasn't trying to take advantage. When I got the call, I was clear on the other side of the store. I needed to rush out of there, and a snail could have crawled faster than that little scooter. I jumped up and ran to the exit. As I ran past the lady at the entrance, I yelled, "Family emergency!" She pointed at me and yelled back, "AHA! I knew it!"

By the time I got home, the firemen and EMTs were arriving. They stabilized him and my wife and son got into the ambulance to go to the hospital. My next door neighbor, a sweet lady we call Nana, came over to sit with my daughter while she slept. As I watched the ambulance drive away, I turned to Nana and just collapsed into her arms. I cried and she cried and she prayed for me. I got in my truck and headed to the hospital.

I dialed my parents and for that 8 minute ride to the ER, a battle ensued. It was all out war. I was in that moment just like I was in that shower. I was battling for my son. I realized in that moment the very best thing I could do for him, as his daddy, as his protector, as his covering, was to just stop and pray. It was to remember whose son he really was, to remember that I am a steward of my little boy, that he isn't mine, and that meant that God was going to take care of him, and that God would see him reach his purpose, whether that meant 100 years on this earth or only two months. My son belonged to God and God was mighty enough to save. My role in that moment was to pray, to war, to battle from a place of knowing that God is in control. So I went to battle. I put on my helmet. I put on my gear. I got my sword and shield and went to battle. The story ends with him being fine after a fight with viral meningitis. We spent a week in the hospital, but he was okay. But my instant response in that moment had to be prayer, not to freak out, because if I can just glass house for a moment, a part of me wanted to freak out. A part of me wanted to go full on Job for a second. "God what are you doing? You give me a son and take him away?!" I had to remember that there is never something going on that is happening too quickly that I can't stop and pray. I know it sounds simple, but we are men who have the Holy Spirit living inside of us. We have time to pray.

The second way we respond is God's Word. If you look into Ephesians 6 and look at the Armor of God, the Sword of the Spirit is the only offensive weapon God has given us. Jimmy Evans has a great book called, "A Mind Set Free." It is a small book, a super quick read, but it is all about using the Sword of the Spirit to fight. When you have a thought, for instance, that isn't pure, responding with another thought that is a happy thought doesn't stop the attack. It isn't going to do anything for you. That is a defensive mechanism, not an offensive one. You have to respond with the offensive weapon, and that is the Word of God. If an impure thought comes into my mind, I need to respond by saying, "You know what, the Bible tells me I am to think about things that are pure and holy, things that are of good repute. I am supposed to renew my mind daily. I have

13

the mind of Christ. Holy Spirit, I ask you to renew my mind. I release you to flush out impure thoughts, and fill me with Heaven's thoughts." In that moment, I am responding with the Word of God and it stops the attack instantly. In my book, "Free," I say the same thing. Behavioral changes only work for a time. The Sword of the Spirit is what changes your heart. You have to find a promise in the Word and stand on it. We have to find a promise in scripture and fight back with it. If the doctor says, "Your kid may have diabetes forever," and the prophetic word we got from Jimmy Evans is "a new bloodline," then I am going to attach the prophetic and scripture together that "life is in the blood," that we are "bought with the blood of Jesus," and stand on these promises, and fight with these promises.

The last way to respond is with power. This is a fight and in a battle, you need power. Like a charger in battle, power gives you the advantage over the enemy. In Romans 8:11, we see that,

> "If the Spirit of him who raised Jesus from the dead dwells in you, he who raised Christ Jesus from the dead will also give life to your mortal bodies through his Spirit who dwells in you."

We can't forget, and this is powerful, that we have the same advantage that Jesus had. I've always looked at Jesus and thought, "Man, what an advantage he had! God AND man!" Think about it. While we have no documentation of this, just imagine that when he was say six years old and Mary told him to clean his room, he didn't roll his eyes or disrespected her once, because that would have disqualified him. Have you ever thought about that? How could Jesus do that? There's an incredible book called, Delighting in the Trinity by Michael Reeves where the author says that Jesus was able to obey so exquisitely because he was so perfectly loved by his Father, his natural reaction was to obey, thereby reciprocating that love. That sounds incredible, but how does this work for us? Well the good news is that if you are filled with the Holy Spirit, you are God and man, too. Jesus said it was better that he go away so he could send the Holy Spirit. Would it be better for me to have Jesus walking along side me, or would it be better for me to have the power that raised him from the dead living inside of me? See, it changes how you fight, because all of the sudden you aren't just a little guy out there wielding a plastic sword, you are a man with the same power that raised Jesus from the dead, that said, "Lazarus come forth," that said, "Let there be light," living inside of you. What does that mean about the fight I am in? All of the sudden I am putting what we talked about at the beginning, that "the battle is the Lord's" into practice and in line with what God has put in my heart and spirit. I have power over the enemy, over the works of the enemy. Everything that Jesus did was incredible, but he said we would do even greater things than these! I'm standing on that! I am going to respond with prayer. I am going to find a promise and I am going to drive that thing home and stand on it until I can't stand anymore, and then I am going to stand on the fact

> **GOD HAS EMPOWERED YOU TO WIN THE VERY BATTLE YOU ARE FACING RIGHT NOW.**

that God has empowered me for the battle I am facing. That is something you really need to hear. The battle you are facing, God has empowered you to win that very battle. We cannot go into it thinking, "Man, I hope I win," or expecting defeat. If God has placed you in a battle, he is going to see you win it, if you will respond in the right way. Be encouraged, as well, that even when you find yourself in a battle that God never intended you to fight, one that you got into all by yourself, and you find yourself in a mess, God will help you. I am convinced that the same God that said in Romans 5:8 that even while we were sinners and enemies of God, he showed his love for us that still he died for us, is the same God that will deliver you from "unauthorized engagements." We see this all throughout the Bible, starting with the first bite of that apple.

Lastly, I want to tell you about Medal of Honor recipient, Roy Benavidez.

In 1965, he was sent to South Vietnam as an advisor to an Army

15

of the Republic of Vietnam infantry regiment. He stepped on a land mine during a patrol and was evacuated to the United States, where doctors at Fort Sam Houston concluded he would never walk again and began preparing his medical discharge papers. As Benavidez noted in his 1981 Medal of Honor acceptance speech, stung by the diagnosis, as well as flag burnings and media criticisms of the U.S. military presence in Vietnam he saw on TV, he began an unsanctioned nightly training ritual in an attempt to redevelop his ability to walk. Getting out of bed at night (against doctors' orders), Benavidez would crawl using his elbows and chin to a wall near his bedside and (with the encouragement of his fellow patients, many of whom were permanently paralyzed and/or missing limbs), he would prop himself against the wall and attempt to lift himself unaided, starting by wiggling his toes, then his feet, and then eventually (after several months of excruciating practice that by his own admission often left him in tears) pushing himself up the wall with his ankles and legs.

His doctor walked in one day with his discharge papers, and Benavidez demanded the doctor tear them up. The doctor responded, "The only way I will tear these up is if I see you walk out that door." Benavidez stood, and with a limp and much pain, walked out the door. The doctor kept his word.

After over a year of hospitalization, Benavidez walked out of the hospital in July 1966, with his wife at his side, determined to return to combat in Vietnam. Despite continuing pain from his wounds, he returned to South Vietnam in January 1968.

On May 2, 1968, a 12-man Special Forces patrol, which included nine Montagnard tribesmen, was surrounded by a North Vietnamese infantry battalion of about 1,000 men. Benavidez heard the radio appeal for help and boarded a helicopter to respond. Armed only with a knife, he jumped from the helicopter carrying

16

his medical bag and ran to help the trapped patrol. Benavidez "distinguished himself by a series of daring and extremely valorous actions... and because of his gallant choice to join voluntarily his comrades who were in critical straits, to expose himself constantly to withering enemy fire, and his refusal to be stopped despite numerous severe wounds, saved the lives of at least eight men." At one point in the battle a North Vietnamese soldier accosted him and stabbed him with a bayonet. Benavidez pulled it out, yanked out his own knife, killed the North Vietnamese soldier and kept going, leaving his knife in the dead soldier's body. While he was attempting to get to a helicopter, and while holding his own intestines in his hand, Benavidez managed to gather every wounded or dead soldier and, with help, load them onto the helicopter. Medics later reported that in his haste to get every man out, he had actually loaded three dead Vietcong soldiers as well. When asked later about that, he simply replied, "I just didn't want to leave anyone." After the battle, he was evacuated to the base camp, examined, and thought to be dead. As he was placed in a body bag among the other dead in body bags, he was suddenly recognized by a friend who called for help. A doctor came and examined him but believed Benavidez was dead. The doctor was about to zip up the body bag when Benavidez spat in his face, alerting the doctor that he was alive. Benavidez in his acceptance speech told the crowd that "it was the luckiest shot I ever made, spitting in that doctor's face."

The six-hour battle left Benavidez with seven major gunshot wounds, 28 fragmentation holes, and both his arms were slashed by a bayonet. He had fragments in his head, scalp, shoulder, buttocks, feet, and legs, his right lung was destroyed, and he had injuries to his mouth and back of his head from being clubbed with a rifle butt. A bullet shot from an AK-47 entered his back and exited just beneath his heart. Benavidez was evacuated to Fort Sam Houston's Brooke Army Medical Center in San Antonio, Texas, and he spent almost a year in hospitals recovering from his injuries.

Benavidez said this when asked why he did what he did, and this is the crux of why I am mentioning this American hero: "And I saw a lot of other patients coming back, limbs missing. I wanted to go back. I was determined 'cause I remember what I was taught at jump school. That old Master Sergeant would tell me, 'Benavidez, quitters never win and winners never quit. What are you?' [I said], 'I'm a winner.'"

If there's anything I want you to get out of this first chapter together, it is this: You are in a battle whether you like it or not, and while you might feel fear, you need to react in faith, because your response is going to determine whether you walk out the victory Jesus has already won. That is my encouragement to you in this moment. As you battle in your own life, how are you responding? Do you have the same drive that led Sgt. Benavidez to do what he was willing to do, he in the natural but you in the spiritual? You need to have a deep-seated devotion to God, your family, devotion to this idea that you won't back down, you won't quit, you won't give up, you won't let the enemy overrun you or your family. You need to stand and battle. Do you have it inside of your spirit that you are not going to leave anyone in your family behind? My favorite Bible verse is Hebrews 12:12-13, which says,

"Take a new grip with your tired hands, strengthen your weak knees, mark out a straight path for your feet, so that those who follow behind you will not become lame, but will be healed."

Am I strengthening my hands, even though it would be easier to give up? Am I strengthening my knees, even though the weight is heavy? Am I marking out a straight path for my feet, knowing that it is God's word that is "a lamp unto my feet and a light unto my path?" Am I marking a straight path for my family, knowing that I am the leader of my home? Am I walkng in such a way that it will bring healing to my family? What is it going to be? Fear or Faith?

This is where I found myself when faced with my daughter's genetic issue. I had to make daily decisions to fight, daily decisions to win. Jesus has already won the battle. Was I going to walk in that or not? I had to chose to respond in faith, not fear. I had to find a promise and stand on it, and rest in the power that God has given me. That is how I had to fight, and that is how I won. I want you to win, too.

Small Group Questions

1. Rulers, authorities, cosmic powers over this present darkness, spiritual forces of evil. How would you describe these enemies that we are fighting?

_____

_____

_____

_____

_____

2. Which front do you think you battle on the most and why? Spiritual, Physical, or the Soul?

_____

_____

_____

_____

_____

3. If you were to arrange the three fronts in their current order in your life, what would it be?

_____

_____

_____

_____

_____

4. What does your prayer life look like right now?

_____

_____

_____

_____

_____

5. How often do you dig into the Word, and do you get anything from it?

_____

_____

_____

_____

_____

6. How do you apply scripture to your life, especially your problems?

_____

_____

_____

_____

_____

7. What does it mean to have power in terms of God's Kingdom?

_____

_____

_____

_____

_____

8. What are you battling at this moment?

_____

_____

_____

_____

_____

9. In which way do you typically respond, fear or faith? Why?

_____

_____

_____

_____

10. What does it mean to stand your ground in the face of the battle?

_____

_____

_____

_____

_____

CHAPTER 2

THE SOLDIER

In this chapter we are going to talk about you, individually, as a soldier, and hit on why it is so important for us to be godly, prepared soldiers before we go into the battle. Consider this from 5 Star General and Secretary of State, George C. Marshall,

> "The soldier's heart, the soldier's spirit, the soldier's soul, are everything. Unless the soldier's soul sustains him he cannot be relied on and will fail himself and his commander and his country in the end."

This is a guy who knew about soldiering. Take a moment and think about that. It is the soldier's spirit and soul that are everything. They drive whether or not the soldier can succeed, and if the soldier can be relied upon. When I read this quote, it hit me because I thought for a second, "If I look at a normal week for me, how many times can I say my family could not have relied on me in a specific moment?" Maybe my son had done something and I was in a moment of frustration and anger rather than love and trying to help shape the foundation that I need to create in him, but I responded instead out of frustration. See, he couldn't have relied on me in that moment. In fact, in that moment I would be literally teaching him something wrong, what not to do. So it really made me stop and think, not so much, "Can I win?" because I know if I do my best to stay focused on Jesus, I know he is going to help me win in spite of my weaknesses, for remember, when we are weak he is strong, but am I a person that my family can rely on? Can my wife put her trust in me? Can she trust me in terms of finances, or faithfulness? Can my kids trust me that when they mess up they can come to me with their problem and get love and reconciliation, forgiveness, grace, and mercy, not a rage monster? That quote really made an impact on me, and I hope it does for you as well.

What about this from former Sergeant Major of the Army, William G. Bainbridge:

> "The core of a soldier is moral discipline. It is intertwined with the discipline of physical and mental achievement. Total discipline overcomes adversity, and physical stamina draws on an inner strength that says drive on."

Look, there has to be this thing within us as men and leaders that makes us drive on when it is hard, when it is difficult. Again I reference Hebrews 12:12-13, which says,

> "So take a new grip with your tired hands and strengthen your weak knees. Mark out a straight path for your feet so that those who are weak and lame will not fall but become strong." (NLT)

When I read this chapter and consider the quote from Bainbridge, I cannot help but see that my willingness to persevere in spite of hardship, in spite of the struggle, has a direct correlation on those who I am leading, namely my family. Their fall as a result of lameness and weakness or their opportunity to become strong is largely due to my willingness to take a new grip, strengthen my weak knees, and mark out a straight path. Even when I am tired of holding on, I take a new grip any way. We have to be focused on that. We all have tough days, and when we have these tough

26

days and seasons, and our ability to keep holding is getting too hard, we have to tap into God's strength. When the knees are wanting to buckle because the weight is too much, we have to tap into God's strength. But there also has to be something in us that drives us to win in spite of it all. Winners keep pushing when all the rest stop. Do you have that drive inside of you? I will fight. I will win. And honestly, that is not something you can develop in the battle. That is something you have to have before you ever step on the battlefield.

This is why it is so important that we understand and make sure that we have what it takes inside, that we are prepared for what is to come. Any army worth its salt is not a singular unit, but an amalgam of individual soldiers upon who rest the integrity and resilience of a military force. It isn't the munitions and equipment that make an army a threat. It is the soldier. None knew this better than General George Washington. Washington often spoke ill of the Revolutionary War militia, which was a voluntary group of laymen, non-soldiers, mainly farmers and local residents. Consider this from the Smithsonian:

> "Some Americans emerged from the war convinced that the militia had been largely ineffective. No one did more to sully its reputation than General Washington, who insisted that a decision to 'place any dependence on Militia is assuredly resting on a broken staff.'

> Militiamen were older, on average, than the Continental soldiers and received only perfunctory training; few had experienced combat. Washington complained that militiamen had failed to exhibit "a brave & manly opposition" in the battles of 1776 on Long Island and in Manhattan. At Camden, South Carolina, in August 1780, militiamen panicked in the face of advancing redcoats. Throwing down their weapons and running for safety, they were responsible for one of the worst defeats of the war."

In all honesty, there have been plenty of times in my life where I have act-ed more like a militiaman than a soldier, times where I have been afraid and rather than stand and fight, I throw down my weapon and run for safety. Perhaps you can understand that in your own life. In Washington's mind, and perhaps ours as well, we see the strength in an army rests in their experience, their will, their drive, and their preparation for the battle. One might think that a militiaman who was an every day guy, a farmer, a business man, that even when an opposing force was coming in to oppress them, that there would be something in them that says, "There's no way I am going to stand here and let you take what I have worked so hard for." But none of that was there. Why? It is because there has to be something inside of us that exists separately from our fleshly nature that drives us to battle like God has called us to do.

The reason I am mentioning these quotes from these heroic men is to help you understand that in military warfare, the strength of the army lies in its soldier. In the exact same way, the strength of your home lies in you. We can talk about God fighting our battles. We can talk about the victo-ry belonging to the Lord. But there is a responsibility upon you to be the soldier you need to be for your family in the midst of this war. The devil wants your family and if you are positioned properly, he will have to come through you to get your family. So if you are not prepared individually, as a man of God, then what is going to happen is your house will be ran-sacked.

Consider Mark 3:24-27.

> "If a kingdom is divided against itself, that kingdom cannot stand. And if a house is divided against itself, that house will not be able to stand. And if Satan has risen up against himself and is divided, he cannot stand, but is coming to an end. But no one can enter a strong man's house and plunder his goods, unless he first binds the strong man. Then indeed he may plunder his house."

You represent your house. You are the strong man. We've heard before what you leave at the cross your children won't have to deal with." Let me take it a step further by saying this, "What you discipline in your life will be disciplined in your home." If prayer is not a discipline in your life, it won't be in your home. If stewardship is not a discipline in your life, it won't be in your home. And on the other side, if immorality is a discipline in your life, it will be in your home. If anger is a discipline in your life, it will be in your home.

> # WHAT YOU ALLOW IN YOUR LIFE YOU GIVE ACCESS TO YOUR HOME, SO BE CAREFUL WHAT YOU ALLOW IN YOUR LIFE.

If you look around your house and see some things that you don't like, habits and actions that you are unhappy with, before you start pointing fingers, take some inventory. Ask yourself, "Is the thing I am seeing in my family that I don't like a result of my lack of discipline in some area?" As the leader of the family, you set the tone for discipline, behavior, and what you want to see thrive in your home. If you want a family of praying people, then you have to be a praying leader. If you want worship to live between your walls, you are the one who sets that tone. What you allow in your life will have open access to your home, so you'd better be very careful what you allow in your life. That is why I believe that what you discipline in you will be a discipline in your home.

Now as a disclaimer, let me say that there are plenty of people out there who have disciplined themselves and disciplined their homes and still have issues. In the over 20 years of ministry I have been involved in, we have seen drastic mistakes from great families. We have to understand that you can do your very best to lead well and people in your home can still make bad decisions. If you don't believe that, then just remember, Jesus had 12 disciples and one of them turned our to be a devil. I am not saying that if you do discipline the right things in your home that your kids will be perfect. We are all responsible for our own actions, no matter what background we've come from. But what I am saying is that if you want

29

to see something in your home, it has to start in you. You can break the generational cycles in your life by doing this.

I have a friend who used to dip chewing tobacco. He had tried to quit before with no success, but one day he found out his high school aged son had started dipping too. He didn't like that, but he was fully aware that he had no grounds to stand on to get his son to stop. He had an addiction, and so he felt like in terms of any addiction his son might have, that he had nothing to stand on to get him to stop, be it snuff, or drinking, or whatever else. He was the strong man and was bound to an addiction, and that addiction had made its way into his home. It was at that moment that he simply surrendered his addiction to God. As he surrendered his addiction to God, he went to speak to his son, who was at that moment playing a video game in his room. He simply told his son, "Look, I have been dipping and I see that it is something that you have picked up. I'm not saying you have to quit, but I wanted you to know that I have surrendered this to the Lord and I am quitting. If you want to quit too, I'd love for you to join me." He walked out and went back downstairs. Thirty minutes later, his son came down, put his snuff on the table and said, "Hey, padre, I don't want this anymore. I want to quit." The result was more than my friend could have imagined. He thought the win would be that he would stop dipping, but in reality, his relationship with his son grew exponentially in that moment.

What could be a better representation of what Jesus was talking about with the strong man? My friend couldn't speak to his son because he himself was bound. We have to understand that you can be bound by anything. Addiction to a substance, pornography, anger, a lot of different things. It is amazing, though, that we can get caught in a mindset where we want to see a difference in our home, but we don't do what it takes to get freedom in our heart first. You have to see the value of your own freedom. It isn't just that you are no longer bound, it is that your family is no longer at risk of a rout due to the thing you refuse to discipline in your life. I pray that gives you encouragement to make a change, get free, so

30

that your family can flourish. So here's a few things you need to know as you prepare.

First, you are the primary target. You need to go ahead and get this in your mind. The enemy is gunning for you and you first. John 10:10 tells us that

> "The thief comes only to steal and kill and destroy."

A soldier knows that the enemy wants to kill him. That should create a fire in the soldier to prepare for that attack. It can be difficult in the heat of battle to process the situation, but when you know going in that your life and the lives of your family are on the line, you prepare. Often times it is not clear, logical thinking that wins the moment, it is the muscle memory you learned in preparation. We know thieves like to come at night in the cover of darkness That makes us get security cameras, outdoor lighting, and a bedside gun as we prepare for the eventuality. Knowing that you are the primary target, and that your family is the thing Satan is trying to destroy, then it should spur you to action to do something to either stop or overcome the attack. You are the primary target.

Secondly, your soil is your responsibility. Just like a soldier is responsible for his training, you are responsible for your own life, actions, etc. Of course the soldier has guides, manuals, instructors, drill sergeants yelling! He has boot camp. Despite this, he still has to take the responsibility to learn what he is being taught. Have you heard of anyone getting kicked out of boot camp? These are people who are unwilling to take responsibility for their training. You have the opportunity for training, too, but you have to be willing to put yourself into a place where you can be trained. If a young man wants to be a soldier, he doesn't just sit at the house expecting soldiering to magically make its way into his mind and body. He puts himself - voluntarily - in a place where he is required to do something. I think this really points to a huge issue today in people called a victim mentality. It is demonic. It says things like, "Well I didn't have a dad to teach me." or "No one has ever cared enough to show me how." I am empathetic to that situation, but that is a victim talking. My dad never had anyone to teach him what it meant to be a good father. His dad died when he was only ten. I asked my dad once before, "How did you learn how to be such a good dad when you didn't have one." He said, "I did have one. God was my dad." See, he put himself - voluntarily - where he could get the training he needed, even if the only place that could be found was in the arms of his Heavenly Father.. Now there were some men who came alongside him and helped him as an adult, Mr. Williams, Mr. Merchant, and they were great helps to my father, but the one who really showed him what being a father meant was God Almighty.

> # SATAN CALLS YOU A VICTIM AND HE WILL REMIND YOU OF IT OFTEN, BUT GOD SAYS YOU ARE A VICTOR.

I am empathetic, but this is a demonic attack against men and anytime you hear someone say, "I didn't have this," or "I didn't have that," it is that victim mentality talking. Satan says you are a victim, and he'll remind you of that often, but God says you are a victor. The only difference between the victim and the victor is how committed you are to making something of yourself, how committed you are to breaking the cycle in your life. There has to be a drive in you to take responsibility for what is going on in your life.

Let me love you enough in this moment to tell you that if you don't know how to do something in your life, find someone who does and submit to them. If your finances are a wreck, find a godly steward and open your books to them. Let them look at your spending. "Well they might know what I am spending my money on." That's right! They will! They will help you make better decisions and learn stewardship. Do you want to win or not? Is scraping by paycheck to paycheck a joy? Get help! If your marriage is in shambles, swallow some pride and see a marriage pastor or Christian therapist. I emphasize Christian-driven counseling only because you need someone who will point you both to Jesus, not just your feel-ngs. Feelings are fickle and untrustworthy. You can't build a marriage foundation on a feeling, but you can on Jesus. I know it against the "macho guy" thing, to go to counseling with your wife, but that mindset is a lie and a trap intended to bind you, the strong man. If you really want to win in life, you have to take responsibility for your own soil.

So what do I mean by your soil? Think of it like a plant. What do plants need? Light. Water. Good soil. God is in charge of the light and the growth. We are in charge of the watering and good soil. Consider what we find in one of Jesus' parables in Matthew 13:1-8.

> "That same day Jesus went out of the house and sat beside the sea. And great crowds gathered about him, so that he got into a boat and sat down. And the whole crowd stood on the beach. And he told them many things in parables, saying: 'A sower went out to sow. And as he sowed, some seeds fell along the path, and the birds came and devoured them. Other seeds fell on rocky ground, where they did not have much soil, and immediately they sprang up, since they had no depth of soil, but when the sun rose they were scorched. And since they had no root, they withered away. Other seeds fell among thorns, and the thorns grew up and choked them. Other seeds fell on good soil and produced grain, some a hundredfold, some sixty, some thirty.'"

So we see here that a sower went out to sow. Some seeds fell along the path. When I see the path, I see the busyness of life. Paths are trampled upon relentlessly so that nothing can grow. It is so easy to get bogged down in the busyness of life and the seed have zero soil in which to root. Some seeds fell on rocky ground. I see this as iniquity. Now there is a difference between iniquity and sin. Sin is missing the mark. I am shooting at the target, I am trying to do the right thing, I just mess up. Iniquity is a habitual sin that you constantly do. It is a sin deep inside of you, and many times they are generational. Alcoholism, sexual immorality, things that you constantly have to fight against. The way you deal with iniquity is

33

the same way you deal with something like an orphan spirit. You have to give it over to the Lord, fight it with the Sword of the Spirit through biblical meditation, and by the power of the Holy Spirit, be set free from it. Again, I highly recommend Jimmy Evan's book A Mind Set Free to learn how to successfully meditate on God's Word so that you can fight. Some seeds fell among thorns. These are the sins, enticements of the world, missing the mark that I mentioned before. And lastly, some seeds fell on good soil and produced.

When I say your soil is your responsibility it is because these are areas you have to deal with in order to make sure your soil is ready for the deposit the Holy Spirit wants to place within you for the sake of your family and your future. You need to know that while the enemy has a target on you, the Holy Spirit has a seed he is wanting to place inside of you. I promise you now, he is not going to put seed inside of unprepared soil.

When my friend quit dipping, he not only connected with his son, he also formed some friendships with men in the church, one specifically, who helped them start to lead a life group. So he and his wife began leading a life group. He found it amazing that after God delivered him from his own addiction, that God brought men into his life through the life group with addictions. He knew that he could not have spoken life into them had he still been addicted himself, but by dealing with his soil and preparing it for the seed the Holy Spirit had for him, he was able to speak life into these men and help them be delivered from their addictions as well. They led life groups for the following eight years. God had a plan for him, but he had to give up that addiction and be unbound.

This literally illustrates this whole idea of discipline. Tending the soil takes discipline. When you plant a garden, it is work. You have to weed it and water it and tend it. You come back into the house with dirt under your fingernails and a sore back from leaning over. Discipline isn't the easiest thing, but here's what you have to understand. Discipline is not you not getting to do something. Discipline is creating a space where the Holy

34

Spirit can work. You can't see giving up an addiction as something you are losing, but rather you are allowing the Holy Spirit to have that space that your addiction was taking up. There's a book called *Celebration of Discipline* that I highly recommend if this is an area where you struggle.

I came across this book after a friend recommended it to me. I have always had a struggle with my physical health, so one day I took my own advice and sought out someone who was disciplined in this area where I wasn't. After spending some time talking about my struggles, he committed to walking with me to see me succeed in getting healthier. The day after I reached out to him, he sent me a message that I'll never forget. He said, "Jason, I'm not looking for you to be perfect today. Just be one step better than you were yesterday." Coming from a performance-driven mindset for so long, this was such a relief. I had always seen this area as pass-fail. I either was a winner or a loser. There was no gray area, and because there was no gray area, there was no such thing as one step better. I think this is what God is looking for out of us. It is going to take time to make sure our soil is ready. You won't get every weed the first day. You may have to deal with rocks in the dirt that have been there for years, but at the end of the day, we have to take responsibility for out lives and our actions. We have to get our hands in our soil and get our soil ready! We have to remember that a soldier that refuses to be trained can't be prepared for battle, that a man who refuses to deal with his soil is one that can't receive what God wants to give him. You need that deposit in order to fight the battles you face, for yourself, your marriage, and your family. Yes, tending the soil takes discipline, but we have to decide: either ignore the soil and be defeated, or deal with the issues, prepare your soil, and win. It is as simple as that.

> **GOD IS NOT LOOKING FOR PERFECTION FROM YOU. JUST BE ONE STEP BETTER TODAY THAN YOU WERE YESTERDAY.**

Lastly, there are three main areas where the enemy will attack you and we find these areas in 1 John 2:15-17, which says,

> "Do not love the world or the things in the world. If anyone loves the world, the love of the Father is not in him. For all that is in the world—the desires of the flesh and the desires of the eyes and pride of life—is not from the Father but is from the world. And the world is passing away along with its desires, but whoever does the will of God abide forever."

Remember, he is trying to bind the strong man to gain access to your house. There is a reason for this attack. If he gets in your home, he can do the most damage. The family unit is a picture of Heaven in the sense that, within the family unit we find identity and purpose. Think of it like this the core of who you were meant to be in this life is not the job you do or the person you marry. It isn't being a father. It isn't found in your purpose or even necessarily to move the Kingdom of God forward. Your primary role in life is to be a son, a son of God, a child of the Most High King. You learn how to be a son in the presence of a father, so when the family unit is broken down, you are unable to learn the very nature and character of God because the example God created to reveal his very nature to you is in shambles. The metaphor is broken because the physical diagram is wrecked. Does that make sense? Satan is attempting to break down the very thing that God created to build godly foundations, to reveal who God really is, thereby helping your family learn what it means to be children of God. God created the family so that you could build foundations in your children and set the next generation up on a higher level. You want your children's floor to be your ceiling. You want the best for your kids. I want to see my kids succeed even where I failed. I want to see my wife walking in confidence and purpose, living a fulfilled life. So it is incumbent upon us to be sure we are strong, the soldiers we need to be because if we are not, then we are allowing the enemy into our homes to ravish our families, leaving us incapable of building the foundations that our families need, and showing them Heaven's example of what relationship should be all about in the first place. If he can only drive a wedge between you and your wife, if he can only create enmity between you and your children, it allows him to create a divided house, a broken relationship with your spouse, and orphans out of your children. This is what is at stake!

So when I talk about you being a good soldier, it isn't some manly, buff thing where we walk around with our chests out. It is because your family and marriage is depending on it. Your family is depending upon your ability to step into the role of a soldier, a husband, a father, a man of God that he has called you to be.

We have to have this drive in us that says, "I am going to be a good soldier no matter what." That means we have to overcome some things. The way I see it, the areas where the enemy attacks the most on are in these three areas.

The first one is the lust of the flesh. I call this our appetite. Men have an insatiable appetite for things. I used to drool over GMC trucks. That was a dream vehicle for me. I would pass our GMC dealer every week and look over there and get all worked up, but then my mind would start thinking, "How can I move these funds here, and do that note there, then maybe I can get one!" I had to stop myself and remind myself that my appetite for a thing doesn't drive me! Now this is just a funny example that we can laugh about, but my goodness, how much do we do that in our lives? How often are we driven by our disgusting appetite, our lust of the flesh?

Galatians 5:19-21 says,

> "Now the works of the flesh are evident: sexual immorality, impurity, sensuality, idolatry, sorcery, enmity, strife, jealousy, fits of anger, rivalries, dissensions, divisions, envy, drunkenness, orgies, and things like these. I warn you, as I warned you before, that those who do such things will not inherit the kingdom of God."

This is what your flesh is vying for you to do. This is what the flesh wants. Galatians 5:17, just a few verses before, says,

> "For the flesh lusts against the Spirit, and the Spirit against the flesh"

Why do I bring that up? Because you need to understand that you are already in a war, but you have to be careful that you don't ignore the war that is going on inside between your flesh and your spirit. One of the best ways to destroy your family is to destroy the soldier, to bind the strong man, and that is what Satan is trying to do. If you allow the flesh to rule your life, it is not only going to go against the Spirit, it is going to allow you to feast upon the appetite that destroys your family.

I have friends who have made moral failures in their marriages by engaging in cheating, and I always think to myself, "What is the value system there that is driving that?" I am not knocking anyone if you have made that mistake, but there has to be a decision in your heart that says, "An orgasm is more valuable to me in this moment than my family." Maybe it isn't the sexual release, but it is the sense of power that you still "have it." That power, at least for a moment in their mind, is more important than their family, more important than the hurt and brokenness they will bring upon their wives, more than the unbridled destruction it will bring into the lives of their children. What is more important than your wife and children? Now listen, there is grace like a river, mercies new every morning, and there are plenty of people who have made that mistake and have sought forgiveness and reconciliation and God has made beauty from the ashes of that experience. When the fall happened, it didn't mean we wouldn't have to endure the results of sin, but God is all about restoring what was broken, so if you have experienced this type of thing, please know there is reconciliation if you will do what it takes. I bring this up, however, to reinforce the truth that your appetite wants you to focus on a very small, quick, fleeting feeling of supposed satisfaction that only brings chaos and destruction in the end. So if I could tell you anything when it comes to the lust of the flesh and your appetite, is to ignore the appetite and feast on the faithfulness. If you are so hungry for something feast on God's faithfulness and be faithful. Feast on God's goodness and be good, not only with your spouse and children, but in every aspect of your life.

The next one is lust of the eyes. I see this as greed. Exodus 20:17 says,

> "You shall not covet your neighbor's house; you shall not covet your neighbor's wife, or his male servant, or his female servant, or his ox, or his donkey, or anything that is your neighbor's."

For instance, the GMC truck of a friend! The lust of the eyes makes you long for what isn't yours. A relationship with another woman won't fix what is broken in your own relationship with your wife. Joel Osteen says this about your spouse,

> "That person God has given you is a gift. They have approximately 80% of what you need. No person has 100%. If you're not careful, you'll focus on the 20% and end up frustrated."

That 20% that you feel is missing, you'll go looking for somewhere else only to find that person can't be 100% for you either. I don't 100% satisfy my wife in every aspect, mainly because, when I have to get cleaned up, I tend to leave my clothes on the floor and not put them in the hamper. My wife would definitely put that in my 20% missing section. But when she eats something in the bed, she leaves the crumbs and plate on my side of the bed. I put that in her 20%. This may be silly, but they are representative of two things. First, your wife was not made to complete you. She was made to be your helpmate. And second, only God can complete you. Be careful you don't start looking elsewhere for the 20% you think is missing at home. Remember what Hebrews 12:1-2,

> "Therefore, since we are surrounded by such a huge crowd of witnesses to the life of faith, let us strip off every weight that slows

us down, especially the sin that so easily trips us up. And let us run with endurance the race God has set before us. We do this by keeping our eyes on Jesus, the champion who initiates and perfects our faith. Because of the joy awaiting him, he endured the cross, disregarding its shame. Now he is seated in the place of honor beside God's throne." (NLT)

We look to Jesus, not our lusts, and if you want honor in your home, then you run your race, look to Jesus, endure what lies on our path as our Champion initiates and perfects our faith!

Keeping up with the Jones' won't make you happy. Be content. Driving your kid thousands of miles every year for 12 year old baseball won't make your own baseball dreams come true. Don't live vicariously through your kid! Show them what really matters! I am not saying don't play ball. Listen, I played baseball my whole life. Spring ball. Summer ball. Fall ball. Texas Select. Travel tournaments. I loved it, but if we had a game on Sunday, I was in church on Sunday morning. My parents wouldn't allow it. We could play late Saturday, we could play Sunday night, but my parents were committed to showing me, in word and deed, that God was first. You have to show your family what is important. You do. You set the tone. You set the bar. You set the expectations. Don't allow what you see to take your eyes off of what matters. Remember, some things are temporal and some things are eternal. One matters way more than the other.

Lastly, there's the pride of life. I see this as pride and arrogance. Proverbs 16:18 tells us,

"Pride goes before destruction, and a haughty spirit before a fall."

James 4:6 says,

"But he gives more grace. Therefore it says, 'God opposes the proud, but gives grace to the humble.'"

God opposes the proud. That is serious. That is an aggressive term. Your opponent is your enemy and there is a divide between you two. The same thing happens between us and God when we are proud. Now, he doesn't want to destroy us, but we create a massive division between us and God with our pride. This is literally the reason we have an enemy to begin with in the person of Satan. His pride is what started this thing off in the first place, and he wants us to follow suit! It is amazing that we see the results of pride in the fallen angels, yet we are so quick to fall into the trap of pride in our own lives, and insanely, think that we will reap different results! Pride is the reason you have an enemy. Pride is the thing that will bring you down the quickest. Honestly, a daily prayer should be, "Show me where pride lives in me." I don't want to take a step if I have pride in my heart. We all know what happens when we get prideful. We mess up, and often times, in a huge way!

So remember, you are the primary target, your soil is your responsibility, and you are going to face personal battles in these three main areas.

So how can we deal with the targeting? We have to prepare for the inevitable. Psalm 144:1-2 tell us,

> "Blessed be the Lord, my rock, who trains my hands for war, and my fingers for battle; he is my steadfast love and my fortress, my stronghold and my deliverer, my shield and he in whom I take refuge."

If you want to train and prepare yourself for the attack that is coming, you have to get close to Jesus. Get close to God and you will find he trains your hands for war and your fingers for the battle. Many times we think, 'God should expect I know what to do by now and how to handle this," but Paul was clear in Philippians 4:6-7 where he reminds us,

> "...do not be anxious about anything, but in everything by prayer and supplication with thanksgiving let your requests be made

41

known to God. And the peace of God, which surpasses all under-standing, will guard your hearts and your minds in Christ Jesus."

Bring everything to God, not matter how big or little, and allow God's peace to wash over you. You will find not only do you have his peace, but that peace will guard you in the midst of the battle!

How can your soil be good? You have to deal with your issues. Consider Matthew 13:23.

"As for what was sown on good soil, this is the one who hears the word and understands it. He indeed bears fruit and yields."

Sometimes you will see things in your life that need to be addressed. It is your responsibility to address them. Sometimes you will have blind spots, which, by definition, are areas of your life that you can't see. You need people, a team, a squad, to help you identify areas that need to be ad-dressed. We need to learn to love people when they help us see - in love and a genuine desire to see me at my best - what needs to be addressed in our lives, because all that is doing is helping us make sure our soil is good!

How can we overcome these areas of attack and prepare ourselves for battle? Galatians 5:16 tells us,

"But I say, walk by the Spirit, and you will not gratify the desires of the flesh."

These desires are the fruits of the flesh, but God desires that the fruits of the Spirit be evident in our lives. We find them in Galatians 5:22-23.

"But the fruit of the Spirit is love, joy, peace, patience, kindness, goodness, faithfulness, gentleness, self-control; against such things there is no law."

This chapter ends with the answer to the question of how do we over-come the attacks of the enemy, and literally covers all three, lust of the flesh, lust of the eyes, and the pride of life. Galatians 5:24-26,

> "And those who belong to Christ Jesus have crucified the flesh with its passions and desires. If we live by the Spirit, let us also keep in step with the Spirit. Let us not become conceited, provok-ing one another, envying one another."

Galatians 5 covers all three attacks with one admonishment: walk in the Spirit.

I pray you see the value in your integrity, honor, and preparation as a soldier. Your family is counting on you. If we're honest, I would bet I am safe in saying that you are counting on yourself, as well. You should. You should want to be the best you can be. It is going to take being serious about your role as the strong man, as the leader of your home, as the man of God he has called you to be. The process of going from civilian to soldier is not an easy one and it is going to take a lot of work and dedi-cation, but you have a God that is for you, a family that believes in you, a church that is there for you, and a calling that is waiting for you. Let's go be all that we can be.

Small Group Questions

1. What does it mean that the strength of an army lies in its soldiers, and how does that relate to you as a Christian soldier?

_____

_____

_____

_____

_____

2. What are ways Satan tries to bind the strong man?

_____

_____

_____

_____

_____

3. Discipline is a huge part of soldiering. What importance does it have to the Christian man?

_____

_____

_____

_____

_____

4. How do you respond, knowing that you are the primary target?

_____

_____

_____

_____

_____

5. How important is it for you as a godly man to seek help when you find a
ack in yourself?

_____

_____

_____

_____

_____

_____

6. How would you describe your soil?

_____

_____

_____

_____

_____

7. How important is a will to fight in a soldier? Explain.

_____

_____

_____

_____

_____

8. Explain how the phrase, "We're not looking for perfection, just one step
better today," makes you feel.

_____

_____

_____

_____

_____

9. What do you see the enemy trying to do in your home right now?

_____

_____

_____

10. Which of the attacks does the enemy levy against you the most, lust of the flesh, lust of the eyes, or pride of life, and why?

_____

_____

_____

_____

_____

11. If there's one thing you could do to make you one step better as a soldier, as the leader of your home, what would it be, and why?

_____

_____

_____

_____

_____

CHAPTER 3

THE ARMY

While in the last chapter, we talked about you as a soldier and how as a soldier, you needed to be prepared, personally, for the battle that was coming. In this chapter, we are going to discuss the army.

They say the strength of a chain is always measured by its weakest link. Similarly, the strength of an army is always measured by its weakest soldier. If you get a line of soldiers marching into the fray and you have one soldier that is scared to death, waiting for the moment to run away, then there's your weak link. So it is clear that the army must be full of soldiers who have been properly trained and mentally, emotionally, physically, and otherwise prepared for the battle ahead. You don't want someone running when the heat gets on.

Much in the same way, the strength of your home lies in the strength of the man leading that home. That would be you, or at least it should be, not your wife, not your children. While it is important that you be sure you are where you need to be in terms of your relationship with God, your spouse, your children, and beyond, and while it is important that you are constantly evaluating your soil, addressing issues that arise, and dedicating yourself to being the best you can possibly be, it is important to understand that this process doesn't happen in a vacuum. It doesn't happen with you on an island by yourself. It can't happen that way. Going from civilian to soldier is a process that is not done alone. You need a team of people.

Between 2000-2001, the US Army released a new slogan that, while intended to appeal to a young millennial demographic, actually had drastic negative impact among current soldiers.

> "As the economy boomed at the turn of the millennium and fewer young enlistees joined the Army, the decision was made to change the Army slogan again. This decision was due to the strategy intended to win over the new era of a younger audience that was much more influenced by technology and advanced forms of media attention. The external support for this advertising mission came from ad agency Leo Burnett, a Chicago-based company whose clients consisted of McDonald's, Nintendo and Coca-Cola. One key element of Leo Burnett's assignment was compiling information about the potential recruits. The agency team literally hit the streets and the World Wide Web to ask 18- to 24-year-old men about their thoughts on joining the Army and what they think when they hear the word 'Army.' With this essential information in mind, the agency created a slogan intended to resonate a strong message of leadership and independence. And so, the new slogan 'An Army of One' was born. Initially, the Army of One slogan was not seen as positive by veterans in and out of the Army, as the Army had always been about teamwork." (Journal of Business Cases and Applications Volume 14, July, 2015)

Team. While I am not a veteran, I cannot see the army functioning in any other way than as a team. The idea of individuality in the military is an odd statement at best. When you go to boot camp, the first thing they do is give you the exact same clothes to wear, put you in identical barracks with identical beds and foot lockers, shave your head bald, and feed you the same training, gruel, and physical exercise for weeks on end. It seems that the Army is actually trying to kill the idea of individuality. This notion is clearly the same idea as this first hand account from Jon Davis, Marine sergeant, Iraq vet, weapons instructor.

"Receiving is a period before training. You arrive at boot camp, but for the first week or so, you don't actually train. You are just doing paperwork to get into the federal documentation system. You will receive all your gear and start your initial process into "getting ready" for boot camp. But it's the way you do it that is important. The entire time you are yelled at, screamed at, hurried, and stressed. But there is more.

From the first moment you arrive, you are now neck-deep in terror. Everything the drill instructor does has purpose; everything. It may seem funny to you, but it is all crucial and instructional in some way. They are being yelled at before they ever set foot off the bus. You can hear this if you begin listening immediately. Within 5 minutes, 200+ individuals with no group training at all have been trained by drill instructions on how to: listen and learn while at boot camp, respond to instruction, stand in formation, and move as a unit. They have also all been read their rights and responsibilities as recruits and in single file moved to a different area. You will not appreciate the magnitude of this. Every word the drill instructor is saying is memorized. No recruit will be physically touched by a drill instructor. In fact, they won't be touched by one, ever. Surprised? This is a ceremony that has taken place every week for every new group of recruits for decades. It is very well-rehearsed and very well-engineered. As I said before, everything a drill instructor does has purpose.

As I said, this is just the first five minutes. There are three more months of this. Later that night, a recruit will do something else that is transformative in a rather impactful way. Why is the haircut so important? It is part of the erosion of individuality. What? Yes, the erosion of individuality. Why should a warrior lose his individuality? It is what makes him special and unique. It is what makes him valuable. Well, that's the problem. Individuality makes them special and unique. It makes them feel that they might be above someone or something else. They are better than the orders they might receive. They are too good for something. Not at boot camp From Day 1, everyone is the same. In fact, during my time, being called "an individual" was an insult as it meant that you were a person who couldn't put the needs of the unit first. Yes, individuality is repressed as they will spend the next three months dressed the same, act the same, and look the same." (www.slate.com/human-interest/2013/03/why-is-boot-camp-so-intense.html)

This is the heart of boot camp, and the key things to focus on here are "Individuality makes them special and unique. It makes them feel that they might be above someone or something else. They are better than the orders they might receive. They are too good for something."

One of the quickest ways to fall into the snare of the enemy is in thinking that you are above or impervious to an attack, or that you are more important that you really are. This mindset will make you put your wants over the needs of the unit, which, in our civilian situation, is our family. Your family is your unit. You are the one leading them. As a man, as a soldier, you have to consider how your actions will affect the family God has given you. You have to be 100% for your family, ready to protect them, fight for them, lead them, to act towards them the way Christ acts towards the church, the way you want him to act towards you. Otherwise, your unit suffers.

The moment you place your needs above your family's needs, you have left them exposed. We see this same thing in the analogy of the soldier, the army, and the battle. If one soldier does something on their own, for their own protection their own safety, their own comfort, they leave the other soldiers exposed. This is the reason I bring up the notion of individuality within a unit. No one is saying we should ignore or look down upon an individual effort in the battle. We all are blown away by the heroism of Medal of Honor recipients. We need the individual effort! But our individual efforts should be in the betterment of our family so we can win, not for our own selfish desires. This is why we are so amazed at the stories of heroism in battle - even the individual efforts. It is because the hero always acts in a way that minimizes his own wants, needs, and safety, for the sake of the unit and/or cause.

This is a lot of talk, but what does that look like in real life? Simple. I shouldn't go make financial decisions based on my wants in that moment that are going to have drastic, negative impacts on my family. I shouldn't create relationships outside of my family that could have a drastic negative impact on my family. You have to think about what you want and need and determine, if you go after that, does it leave your family exposed to the attack of the enemy?

In men, we often see this attempt to be this superhero, justifying an action by saying it is for their family, but really, it is for their glorification, to make themselves feel better. So what this does to me is make me evaluate my own life, what I am doing, and ask, "Am I acting out in selfishness, or am I really thinking about my unit, my family?"

> **ONE OF SATAN'S BEST TRAPS FOR THE STRONG MAN IS THE TRAP OF ISOLATION.**

Individuality can be very dangerous. It can make a man isolate himself. One of Satan's best traps for the strong man is the trap of isolation, or this idea that you can go this alone. "You don't need people checking in on you. You don't have to ask for help or admit failure or be vulnerable." In fact, these are seen as weaknesses in a man. We hear about a man crying and we think, "What a wuss!" This couldn't be farther from the truth.

Consider what Proverbs 18:1 says,

"Whoever isolates himself seeks his own desire; he breaks out against all sound judgment."

This verse literally equates isolation to selfishness! So let me say that if you are in a place right now where you feel isolated and alone, I am not saying that the isolation is necessarily your fault, but staying that way is. It is on you to reach out for help. It is on you to find some people to build you up. I know you may have tried that and been hurt. The truth is, people are not perfect. People hurt people. Most people aren't trying to be malicious. They respond to you out of their own hurts. But to get out of this isolation, we have to reach out and find some men in our lives to help get us through, to help us fight.

God was clear on this in Genesis 2:18 when he says,

"It is not good that the man should be alone."

Now in the context, God was talking about a spouse, but honestly, if you aren't including your spouse in what is going on in your world, in decisions, in situations you are dealing with, you are erring. You need to include your wife. She needs to know what is going on in your heart, mind, and life. Now, I've mentioned before that as men, we are to take the brunt of the attack, the pain, swallow the pride first, etc. I don't think your wife should carry the load you are carrying. I don't want her to go to bed stressed about finances, but if I am stressed about finances, I need to talk to my spouse. After all, God created her, not to bear the entire load, but to be my helpmate. Isolation, individualism will make you try to bear it all alone, and that is just not what God created the relationship with your spouse for. So let me encourage you that if you aren't including your wife in on what is going on in your heart, you are isolating yourself. She is your helpmate, not one of your children, and I promise I have never heard of a woman who thinks her husband a weakling for baring his soul to her!

ndividuality can also make you think that the battle is something you have to do alone. It is not good for man to be alone in terms of a relationship with a wife, but it is also not good for man to be alone in the battle. Let's look to David in his battle against Goliath in 1 Samuel 17:31-51.

"When the words that David spoke were heard, they repeated them before Saul, and he sent for him. And David said to Saul, 'Let no man's heart fail because of him. Your servant will go and fight with this Philistine.' And Saul said to David, 'You are not able to go against this Philistine to fight with him, for you are but a youth, and he has been a man of war from his youth.' But David said to Saul, 'Your servant used to keep sheep for his father. And when there came a lion, or a bear, and took a lamb from the flock, I went after him and struck him and delivered it out of his mouth. And if he arose against me, I caught him by his beard and struck him and killed him. Your servant has struck down both lions and bears, and this uncircumcised Philistine shall be like one of them, for he has defied the armies of the living God.' And David said, 'The Lord who delivered me from the paw of the lion and from the paw of the bear will deliver me from the hand of this Philistine.' And Saul said to David, 'Go, and the Lord be with you!'

Then Saul clothed David with his armor. He put a helmet of bronze on his head and clothed him with a coat of mail, and David strapped his sword over his armor. And he tried in vain to go, for he had not tested them. Then David said to Saul, 'I cannot go with these, for I have not tested them.' So David put them off. Then he took his staff in his hand and chose five smooth stones from the brook and put them in his shepherd's pouch. His sling was in his hand, and he approached the Philistine.

And the Philistine moved forward and came near to David, with his shield-bearer in front of him. And when the Philistine looked and saw David, he disdained him, for he was but a youth, ruddy and handsome in appearance. And the Philistine said to David, 'Am I a dog, that you come to me with sticks?' And the Philistine cursed David by his gods. The Philistine said to David, 'Come to me, and I will give your flesh to the birds of the air and to the beasts of the field.' Then David said to the Philistine, 'You come to me with a sword and with a spear and with a javelin, but I come to you in the name of the Lord of hosts, the God of the armies of Israel, whom you have defied. This day the Lord will deliver you into my hand, and I will strike you down and cut off your head. And I will give the dead bodies of the host of the Philistines this day to the birds of the air and to the wild beasts of the earth, that all the earth may know that there is a God in Israel, and that all this assembly may know that the Lord saves not with sword and spear. For the battle is the Lord's, and he will give you into our hand.'

When the Philistine arose and came and drew near to meet David, David ran quickly toward the battle line to meet the Philistine. And David put his hand in his bag and took out a stone and slung it and struck the Philistine on his forehead. The stone sank into his forehead, and he fell on his face to the ground.

So David prevailed over the Philistine with a sling and with a stone, and struck the Philistine and killed him. There was no sword in the hand of David. Then David ran and stood over the Philistine and took his sword and drew it out of its sheath and killed him and cut off his head with it. When the Philistines saw that their champion was dead, they fled."

Let me draw some points out of this that will help us as we understand how to work with our unit, what I am calling our family, and with the army, which is what I am calling the band of brothers with whom we go to battle.

First, David was not alone and he was not isolated. When we read the story of David and Goliath, this image is painted that it was David and

56

his sling against Goliath and his army. This is the imagery that we always see, even in the cover of this book! This is not entirely true. David had an army behind him as well as before him. You need to understand that while you may have a giant in front of you with an army behind him, you also have an army available to you if you only tap into it.

The last thing you need to think when you are walking across the valley to face your giant is that you are all alone and you have to do it on your own. David confessed that, first, the battle is the Lord's. We need to do that as well. "God this is your battle. I am just following your leadership." But secondly, David didn't deny the army behind him. Not only did he recognize God was there to fight, he recognized that the ones Goliath was defying was the Army of the Living God, the guys standing behind him! We might see a lone soldier facing a giant and an army, but David didn't see that. He saw an army before him and an army behind him. You need to see that, too. Never go into the battle thinking you are alone. If you feel that way right now, take a moment and get help!

Next, David did not rush into the battle without support. David was brought to Saul before he stepped onto the field. David got permission before stepping onto that field. I am not saying you have to get permission before you fight the enemy, but you need to be sure you are allowing yourself the chance to strategize before the battle. You do this by being willing to let others speak into your life. Not just anyone, but let someone.

Saul didn't have a lot of support to offer, but David made sure he did it the right way, allowing himself to get counsel, to get help, before he walked into the battle. There is rarely a battle that comes upon you so quickly that you can't get help before you start swinging a sword. Be sure that when you smell the battle in the air and see the army marching over the horizon, you stop and get support.

Also, David didn't try to be someone else. Saul tried to dress David in his own armor. David was short and Saul was reportedly head and shoulders above everyone else. Imagine that moment when David tried walking around in Saul's armor! The armor would have never fit. Be careful you aren't trying to fight like someone else, with someone else's armor, someone else's technique. God made you for the battle you would face. God trained David in the field for the battle he would face, and believe it or not, God will use what you have learned in your life to help you fight the giant before you. You will be blown away at the stuff you use to fight the battles, stuff you thought was worthless, even the sin from your past. The little battles you face on a daily basis, the lions, the tigers, the bears, are really just training for the giants you will slay one day!

> **IF YOU WANT TO WIN THE BATTLE, IT TAKES THE SWORD OF THE SPIRIT.**

David didn't have all the weapons he needed. We are blown away by David's skill with the sling and stone, but the sling and stone didn't kill Goliath. It was a sword. If you want to win the battle, it takes the Sword of the Spirit in action in the fight. David didn't bring a physical sword into the battle, but he did bring a sword! He brought the Word of the Lord, and before he made a physical strike against the giant, he struck with the Word. This should be an encouragement to us, that before we swing the physical sword, that we swing the spiritual one.

Now remember, David didn't have a physical sword in the battle. That would make any man feel unprepared for the fight. Yet David went anyway. Don't be afraid to go into a battle even if you don't have everything you need. Sometimes battles come and you have to go with what you have. You might not know a verse to fight with on a specific situation. Just fight with the ones you know! But the truth is, when you are living for God and you are focusing on doing things his way, God will provide all your needs, even in the heat of battle. You'll find what you need laying at the side of the giant you just took down. Faith, like with Abraham, will take you up the mountain, and God's love for you and his desire to see you win will provide the ram in the thicket. Trust him in the midst of it all.

Something else, David did not defeat the army in front of him. The army behind him did. This is huge because it reinforces the truth that you are not alone in the fight. There are times when you have to muster more courage and faith than those who are standing around you. Sometimes you will be David in a sea of Israelites and you will need to walk in faith so that others will believe. But sometimes you will be an Israelite, scared, staring down at a David, beginning to believe that you can fight too. In the army you will have both. Sometimes your faith will be so high that you will want to charge hell with a water pistol, but sometimes your faith will be non-existent. That is why you need your army. When your faith is high, you share it. When your faith is low, you get some from others.

David's courage gave the army the courage it needed to attack. Your courage in your family may be the very thing that your family needs to stand and fight, too. It might be the very thing one of your brothers needs to see to encourage him to fight, too. Sometimes you are going to face battles that you can handle, but most times, just like David in this story, you need the army behind you to defeat the army before you. David killed a giant, but the Israelites won the battle. You are in some form of battle now, and if not now, you will be. Look around you. Godly men, an army with you, is what is going to help you to win the battle!

The moral here is two fold: don't be afraid to fight the enemy, but be sure you have an army behind you. I cannot stress enough the value of having a team. Granted, the input from Saul and his men wasn't so great. Don't forget they were terrified too. But David's biggest issue in that moment was not Saul's advice or armor. It was a giant who was defying God. It was an enemy trying to ravage Israel. David wouldn't back down.

Let me ask you this: what armies coming against your home will flee right now if you took that same bulldog faith David exhibited and marched into the field to slay that giant? As a follow up: what army do you have behind you that will be ready when the sword falls to defeat the army before you?

Soldier, you need both. You need the individual, faith-driven, courage filled effort to walk into the battle when no one else will, and you also need the support of an army of men who are willing to battle.

So let's talk for a few minutes about why you need a team. First, the team kills pride. One of my personal core values is humility. Specifically, humility says everyone needs a team. We weren't created to live life alone, the body of Christ is beautiful and powerful when working together. A team mindset will push you towards humility because is makes you recognize that you are not perfect, that you don't have all the answers, and that alone, you have a lower ceiling than God intended for you. A team will move you into a place where you are not trying to do everything on your own in your own strength.

This is a huge problem with men. We try to do everything out of our own strength. We are big, buff, manly men who don't need help, we don't need input, we don't need a team. What a lie! Watch how fast you crash and burn thinking like that. This is where the enemy wants you. The team will kill this mindset in us. You can't do everything. You aren't strong enough. You need help!

That is why the second thing is so important: the team provides support. Because your strength is limited, you must tap into things that are outside of your self for additional strength. Your first tap is always God. If he isn't then you have an idol. He should be the first tap. Consider 2 Corinthians 12:9-11,

> "'My grace is sufficient for you, for my power is made perfect in weakness.' Therefore I will boast all the more gladly of my weaknesses, so that the power of Christ may rest upon me. For the sake of Christ, then, I am content with weaknesses, insults, hardships, persecutions, and calamities. For when I am weak, then I am strong."

I almost want to wake up in the morning and ask God to quickly get me to my weakness so I can walk in his strength. At one point in my life, I had a serious issue with this. My senior pastor thought I had something called high-functioning depression. I was depressed, to be honest. I didn't know why, but something wasn't right. I started seeing a therapist. What it all boiled down to was the fact that I was trying to do everything in my own strength. A lot of times emotional issues are rooted in our not believing in God's truth. That is what it was for me. When I would get to the end of my own strength, I would try to tap into more strength in me. All I was doing was using myself as fuel and I was getting burnt out. I was not tapping into the strength that comes from God when my weakness begins. I just wasn't believing and doing the Word.

Your second tap is your spouse. Including your spouse in your battle is important. Imagine how David's courage would have been boosted even higher had Saul not said, "Go, and the Lord be with you," but instead, "Go, and the Lord be with you, and David, I believe in you!" Now, Saul was not David's spouse, but imagine you come to your spouse with a battle you are facing and she responds to you with, "I believe in you. I am for you." How will that help you? The support will be like a handkerchief in the helmet like in the knights of old. You will be so pumped you'll try to fight two giants! There are a lot of battles I face on a regular basis, and I don't always tell my wife every detail because I don't want her to stress, but one of the best things you can do is to bring your wife into your world and allow her the opportunity to speak life into you, to support you, to be a tap of strength in your life as your helpmate.

Your first tap is God, your second is your wife, and your third tap is your army. You need a squad, a team, a group of men who love you, love God, know you, know God, and who have your best interest in mind. Sometimes your battle might be with your spouse. Then go to your team. Ask for insight. Get them to show you the blind spots. And then listen to their advice. And be sure you aren't telling your army the side you want them to hear. Be honest about your situation and allow them to give you guidance.

You need to know that they may reveal a blind spot to you. My team have revealed blind spots in my life. My first reaction was to defend my actions. Can I lovingly tell you to stop doing that? Don't try to defend it. Swallow your pride and tell them, "Thanks for helping me." Be willing to receive counsel from people in your army because they are trying to help you.

Proverbs 11:14 tells us,

> "Where there is no guidance, a people falls, but in an abundance of counselors there is safety."

Why does it say "a people falls?" When I read it, I thought, "Oh that is my family." When you operate without guidance, watch out, because it might be the downfall of your family.

Next, the team provides accountability. One of the best tools you can have in your corner is a friend who is willing to say in love, "This is a problem and you need to address it." Proverbs 27:6 tells us,

> "Faithful are the wounds of a friend; profuse are the kisses of an enemy."

How can a wound be faithful? And from a friend? Better a real friend tell you something that hurts but that you need to hear, rather than a so called friend tell you what you want to hear and the pain really come.

Your team will question your social media activity, your inputs like TV and movies and music, your past habitual sins and how well you are responding to temptation, your dedication and progress towards goals and purposes. It might mean relinquishing some perceived freedom, but the accountability actually provides freedom! Like a marriage, a team requires boundaries, but the boundaries provide more freedom. I am happier married than I ever was while dating. The rules of marriage are a comfort to me and they give me freedom to fully love the one I have chosen. In the same way, my team holds me accountable, but that accountability allows me to go further than I ever thought possible.

Lastly, team is a kingdom term. What is the Kingdom? Romans 14:17,

> "For the kingdom of God is not a matter of eating and drinking but of righteousness and peace and joy in the Holy Spirit."

Look, the best way to encourage righteousness and peace and joy in the Holy Spirit in your life and in your family is by seeking first the Kingdom of God. You will never better engage the Kingdom of God in your life or in your family than when you are completely engaged in the local church and with a godly team. This is why team is a kingdom term. The team is a tool God has given us to get us constantly seeking the Kingdom so that we can make sure our family is seeking the Kingdom.

At the end of the day, your brothers in arms need to be able to trust you in the battle, but you need to be able to trust them as well. When we are operating together as a team, we seek after God's kingdom being established in our lives and in our families. The truth is that you do not have all that it takes to win every battle, but within your relationship with God, your spouse, and your army, you have access to it. It is incumbent upon you to abandon the idea that you have to muscle through on your own. You might have to muscle through some things, but never on your own! When you don't know, ask someone who does. When you can't do, find someone who can teach you. When your faith is low, borrow some from your team. When the struggle is too much, forget your pride, and ask for help. The fatal flaw of man is not in his weakness but in his unwillingness to ask for help.

Think about it like this: How would the world be different today had Adam, rather than sit by and watch his wife bite that apple, rather had simply said, "God, we are being tempted and we don't know what to do. This is not your best for us. We need help." True, someone along the way might

63

have messed it up, but in that moment, the God of Heaven with his army of angels would have rushed to their aid.

It was not good for Adam to be alone. You either. Get a team. Find your army. Forget this idea that you are an army of one. You need the army behind you to defeat the army in front of you. Let's win.

Small Group Questions

1. What is the role of your team in terms of your life and your family?

_____

_____

_____

_____

_____

2. How does your individual integrity and character impact your family?

_____

_____

_____

_____

_____

3. How can a team help you be a better man, husband, father?

_____

_____

_____

_____

_____

4. Do you feel alone and or isolated in your life right now? Why?

_____

_____

_____

_____

5. Do you feel overwhelmed by the battle in front of you?

_____

_____

_____

_____
_____

6. How are you tapping into your team right now to help you win?

_____
_____
_____
_____
_____

7. What percentage of the time are you tapping into your own strength? Why?

_____
_____
_____
_____
_____

8. If there was one thing you could change about you in terms of team, what would it be?

_____
_____
_____
_____
_____

9. Who are three people on your team? Do they know they are your team, and do they know they can talk to you about anything?

_____
_____
_____
_____
_____

10. Give an example of a time when a team helped you battle.

_____

_____

_____

_____

_____

CHAPTER 4

PEACETIME

In this chapter, we are going to discuss how we do things in peacetime. Peacetime and wartime are very different moments. Not every season of your life will be embroiled in a battle, so it is monumentally important that we stay engaged during peacetime simply for the fact that, while you may not be in a battle this second, one is on the horizon. There is always a battle around the bend! That isn't meant to be a discouragement, but the truth. It is important that you be ready for the battle when that moment comes.

In light of that, I spent some time looking into how our US Military operates during peacetime. Here is what David B. Wright, former Gunnery Sergeant at U.S. Marine Corps, had to say.

"It is during peace time that our Soldiers, Marines, Sailors, Airmen, and Coast Guardsman, do their most vital and important service to our nation of their entire service. It is easy to recognize the sacrifices they make during war and combat, but far less so in times of peace. This is when they diligently put in long arduous hours of training to perfect the lessons learned from the last and prior wars. This is when they test, develop, and improve those lessons for the next war, in all possible environments and conditions they may

69

face. It is far harder to motivate and maintain the proficiency of our warriors during peacetime than in war, but this is the time that it is vital to our nation's survival.

It is during times of peace that the next war is won or lost by dedicated men and women putting in these long arduous hours here in our nation, at sea, in the air, and in foreign places. They are the monks who proudly, reverently, with respect and dedication, keep our nation's candle burning."

We often think of the battle as only the engagement, the hand to hand combat, the actual fight, but we have to understand that the battle doesn't begin when the first arrow. It begins long before, during peacetime. It is always during peacetime that things begin to escalate. If you have people good honorable people leading you, then you would hope they are reaching for peace before they are reaching for war. I think of the Cuban Missile Crisis in October of 1962. You can love or hate the Kennedy family, but I think we can all agree that, had the Kennedy brothers, along with the team of people around them, not sought peace as aggressively as they did, we might not be alive today. If you really dig into the history of how close we were to full out nuclear war, you will see how incredibly scary and dangerous it really was. Had not a back channel of communication outside of the normal diplomatic methods been created, then we would have been in nuclear war. There is this incredible move called Thirteen Days that tells the story of the Cuban Missile Crisis. It is incredible, but was it the most amazing is how it depicts the intense desire and incredible actions of those involved - both Americans and Russians - to seek peace rather than war. It is a great movie, but it highlights a great point: peacetime is nice, but it takes hard work to keep it, and it is during peacetime that the attacks are formulated.

During that time of peace, even in your life, things can begin to escalate, so it is important to take some time to discuss what we need to be doing in order for peace to prevail, and to prepare for the battle on the horizon.

70

Every one of us is probably going through something small. I'll call them skirmishes. They aren't full out battles, but they are enough to affect peacetime. Some can last a few minutes, others a few days, yet they are different from a battle. For the most part, we get to experience a lot of peace in our walk with God. If you are living for the Lord and doing what he has told you to do, diligently seeking his Kingdom first, there is a level of protection that you get to experience just because you are living for the Lord. In terms of your money, if you are tithing, there is a level of protection that comes with that. That is a side benefit of the covenant you have with God in terms of your finances. God blesses the 90% when you are in covenant with the 10%, and you will find it goes further than the 100%. Why? It is because of the blanket of protection that is provided by him as a result of your covenant and obedience. The Bible talks about how the Lord will go before you, he'll go along side you, he is above you, he will be beneath you, he even has your six, so you are completely surrounded by God when you are operating in that covenant relationship with him! There is a level of protection that comes with your relationship with Jesus Christ. As a result of this relationship, he takes many of the attacks that the enemy throws at us. This is also why you need to submit to a spiritual authority in your life. For most of us, that means a pastor or a pastoral team. This isn't so they can control you, but so that they can provide a layer of protection for you. I think of the Iron Dome in Israel. The Iron Dome is an anti-missile defense system that automatically watches the skies to detect incoming enemy missiles, and then blasts them out of the sky before they can inflict damage. This is what you get when you are in covenant with God.

So let's look over some things we need to remember during peacetime so that we can be ready when the battle comes to our door.

First, be fit. Don't let peacetime get you out of fighting shape. 1 Samuel 17:32-36 says,

"And David said to Saul, "Let no man's heart fail because of him.

71

Your servant will go and fight with this Philistine." And Saul said to David, "You are not able to go against this Philistine to fight with him, for you are but a youth, and he has been a man of war from his youth." But David said to Saul, "Your servant used to keep sheep for his father. And when there came a lion, or a bear, and took a lamb from the flock, I went after him and struck him and delivered it out of his mouth. And if he arose against me, I caught him by his beard and struck him and killed him. Your servant has struck down both lions and bears, and this uncircumcised Philistine shall be like one of them, for he has defied the armies of the living God."

I want to note that David was simply doing his job when the animals attacked. He was not intentionally preparing for battle, but he was staying fit for battle, keeping in fighting shape as he protected his sheep. It is imperative that we as men over our homes stay in fighting shape because at any moment, Satan is going to send a lion or bear to attack us. We need to make sure we are ready to face those attacks. Being fit doesn't mean roaming around looking for a fight. This is not about being a bully looking to whoop someone, but it does mean using the little skirmishes along the border to help prepare you. Many times, God will send difficulties in your life to work some things out of you or prep you for something ahead. Maybe he needs to get an attitude out of your system, so he uses those little skirmishes into your life that teach you what to do, to keep you fit and ready to fight when the enemy does come. Maybe you get a bill that, instead of being $200, it is $500. Now, that is a skirmish because what that does is makes you decide in that moment, "Who am I going to trust right now? My own ability to make the difference, or trust God that he will meet my needs according to his riches in glory?" That is a skirmish. It helps prepare you for the battle to come.

1 Timothy 4:7-8 says,

"Have nothing to do with irreverent, silly myths. Rather train your-

self for godliness; for while bodily training is of some value, godliness is of value in every way, as it holds promise for the present
life and also for the life to come."

When we talk about staying fit you might thing physically, which is important. You need to live to lead. Paul referenced physical fitness and the fact
that there is a benefit to the physical side of fitness, but it is minimal in
comparison to the spiritual fitness that we need to have if we are to overcome the works of the enemy in our lives. You need to be fit, but be fit for
godliness more than anything. This is why we train.

The second thing is to be vigilant. Peacetime can make things seem okay
so you let your guard down. 1 Peter 5:8 says,

> "Be sober-minded; be watchful. Your adversary the devil prowls
> around like a roaring lion, seeking someone to devour."

In your moment of weakness, the enemy will attack. Romans 8:26 says,

> "Likewise the Spirit helps us in our weakness..."

Hebrews 4:15-16 tells us,

> "For we do not have a high priest who is unable to sympathize
> with our weaknesses, but one who in every respect has been
> tempted as we are, yet without sin. Let us then with confidence
> draw near to the throne of grace, that we may receive mercy and
> find grace to help in time of need."

Like I mentioned earlier, one of the biggest problems we face as men is
that, when we get in our weakness, we don't ask for help. A part of being
vigilant is recognizing when you need to get help! It isn't enough to spot
the enemy prowling around. It isn't enough to be able to identify something going on in your house. This is what we normally think of when we

think of being vigilant. Yes, we need to be vigilant of what is going on in our homes, but we also need to be vigilant in terms of our own walk with God, our own lives. Satan attacks in the weak moments, not when you are at full strength. We see this a lot in sexual temptation. When we are tired or in a weak moment in our lives, Satan comes with the temptation. Be sure that you are being vigilant in your own life, just like you are in your home.

Maybe your kid comes in one day with an attitude and you think, "Wait a minute, where did that come from?" You need to be vigilant enough to see that, because in peacetime, when everything seems okay, you can let your guard down, and the moment you do that, there comes the enemy. He is always looking for a weak spot in your life, in your home, and trust me, he will find it! The enemy knows you, He studies your reactions. He watches what you do and how you respond to stimuli. He will let a good looking woman walk across your path just to see if you react, because if you do, then he will send something stronger to tempt you. "If he reacted to that, I wonder what this will do."

Peacetime can be dangerous. We can get complacent. You can be having a great relationship with your wife and kids. The job is great. Everything seems fine. Here is what I've found. When I am having a great relationship with my wife and everything is rolling well, the enemy tries to attack me with sexual immorality. A thought. An image in my mind. Something to

> **BE CAREFUL YOU DON'T ALLOW IN PEACETIME WHAT YOU WOULDN'T ALLOW IN THE BATTLE.**

tempt me with a sin that I struggled with in my past. In that moment I have to be vigilant to realize that one of the reasons my wife and I are doing so well right now is because I am keeping myself and my mind pure, that I am NOT thinking about that junk! I've been focusing on my wife, not some fantasy the enemy is trying to lure me into. We have to be sure to keep our focus on the right thing.

Be careful you don't allow in peacetime what you wouldn't allow in the battle. Look, this doesn't mean no fun in your life. I realize a soldier doesn't have down time outside the wire on a mission like they do inside the wire at the base. In the same way, when we are in the heat of battle, we don't lolly-gag around, but when we are in peacetime and everything is going great, have a good time! It doesn't mean no fun, but it does mean no compromise in your life. Don't allow the peacetime fun to allow peacetime compromise. One good thing you might ask yourself in this moment is this: are there some compromises in my life right now that I am allowing just because it is peacetime? Compromises look like not being faithful to pray and read your Bible every day, not making a conscious effort every day to spend time with your spouse and kids, etc.

The third one is to be practiced. Joshua 1:8 says,

> "This Book of the Law shall not depart from your mouth, but you shall meditate on it day and night, so that you may be careful to do according to all that is written in it. For then you will make your way prosperous, and then you will have good success."

Success and prosperity in your life are tied to how much of the Word of God you ingest and live. So let me say "be practiced" like this: Swing your sword every day. Read the word. Memorize the word. Train and then practice and then do it again. Here's why: what you know in peacetime you'll remember in the battle.

This is the muscle-memory stuff. The last thing you want to do is to go out to battle and either you or someone to the right or left of you has not been practicing their sword play. In the movie Gladiator, at the first gladiator battle, there is a giant gladiator tied to a little frail man who is crying in the corner. No one wants the scared, unpracticed guy next to him. You want the giant, seasoned, practiced gladiator next to you. If you want that for you, make sure that you are that for the person next to you. You need to make sure you have the Word inside of you so that when the battle comes, you can swing your Sword with excellence and skill. Maybe you have certain areas where you know the enemy will attack you or your family, like sexual immorality or rejection, etc. You need to find Bible verses that specifically speak to the areas of focused attack in your life and family so that you can respond well with your sword. This is what it means to be practiced. A great tool for this is www.openbible.info. You can go to a Google search and type, "What does the Bible say about _____?" You fill in the blank with whatever you want to know. Maybe it is fear or anxiety. Every verse in the Bible that talks about that subject will show up in the search. It is a great tool to learn Bible verses based on a topic. Use this tool to learn these verses, and that is how you will practice. What you learn in peacetime you will do in the battle.

The fourth one is be mindful. There are at least 31 verses that address why Jesus came to Earth, verses like, "Jesus came to earth...and the Son of Man has come that..." This is important because, even Jesus, was constantly reminding himself and others why he was here. We see an example in Mark 10:45.

> "For even the Son of Man came not to be served but to serve, and to give his life as a ransom for many."

Don't forget why you are fighting. Satan, your enemy, wants to kill, steal, and destroy you, your marriage, and your family. He wants to ruin you and drag you to hell. You can't forget what you are fighting for, yourselves, your marriages, your families. Be sure that the next time you see your wife and kids you remind yourself, "This is why I am fighting. This is why I am dedicated to being the best I can be. This is why I will deal with things in my own life that are not holy, not pleasing to the Lord because these people depend on me. I am the strong man. I need to make sure I am where I need to be with God because they are who I am fighting for!" We can't forget what it takes to win, and that is one thing. It isn't how manly you are, not how holy you are. It takes the one who has already won the battle, Jesus Christ. He is what it takes to win!

We also need to be mindful that the enemy is preparing his next attack, too, Ephesians 6:11 tells us,

> "Put on the whole armor of God, that you may be able to stand against the schemes of the devil."

What are schemes? A scheme is a systematic plan or arrangement for attaining some particular object or putting a particular idea into effect. Satan is scheming while you are in peacetime. He wants into your home and he will do whatever it takes to get in. Be mindful of this fact. I think it is imperative that we realize that, just like Jesus reminded himself and his followers why he was here, that we remind ourselves on a daily basis why we are fighting, who we are fighting for, and what we need to win.

Lastly, be a peace keeper. While researching our US Military during peacetime, I discovered this: The primary role of the US Military during peacetime is encapsulated in the acronym MOOTW, which is Military Operations Other Than War. The US Military MOOTW focuses on deterring war, resolving conflict, promoting peace, and supporting civil authorities in response to domestic crises. Listen, I don't mean keep peace with Satan. Here's what I mean: you give Satan a space to operate when you allow strife in your home. Be a peacemaker in your home. Diffuse situations with grace and mercy. Mediate problems with wisdom. Find common ground when problems arise. This will mean you swallow pride at times. This will mean you go above and beyond. This will mean balancing truth and grace. This is hard because there are times when you want to just drop the hammer, but hammers can be destructive if they aren't hitting a nail! And too much grace will allow compromise. But when you mix truth and grace together, you create a space where the Holy Spirit can enter and allow peace to rule in your home. You can't go in with the guns blazing causing more damage that if you had let it go! So we have to be sure we ask the Holy Spirit to help us in these moments to do the right thing. When there is a problem, we want godly solutions, not fleshly ones. Remember, what you want to see in your home starts with you.

Peacemaking is hard, though! Consider this from Randolph D. Brandt.

> "It's peace that's hard, despite its logic. People have to give up too much for peace. Peace is much harder than war, and it takes infinitely more courage."

Romans 12:18 reminds us,

> "If possible, so far as it depends on you, live peaceably with all."

What you do in peacetime you will do in the battle, so make sure that when everything is right in your life, your marriage, your family, that you are continually focusing on God, living for him, and being fit, vigilant, practiced, mindful, and a peace maker. The enemy is going to attack. It isn't a question of if, but of when, and if you aren't feeling attacked right now, rest assured that he is planning his next assault. He wants a way into your house. Be sure that when everything is fine that you don't let your guard down and allow the enemy to bind you, the strong man.

Small Group Questions

1. What are some ways the enemy attacks us during peace time?

_____

_____

_____

_____

_____

2. What are some ways we let our guard down during peace time?

_____

_____

_____

_____

_____

3. How have the little skirmishes in your life prepared you for battles?

_____

_____

_____

_____

_____

4. What does it mean to swing your sword every day?

_____

_____

_____

_____

_____

5. Why is remembering why you are fighting so important?

_____

_____

6. How do you know when to seek peace and when to go to battle?

_____
_____
_____
_____
_____

7. What are some things we might allow in peacetime that will hurt us in the battle?

_____
_____
_____
_____
_____

8. How can complacency in peacetime kill you in the battle?

_____
_____
_____
_____
_____

9. How big of a deal is having the Word in you before the battle begins?

_____
_____
_____
_____
_____

10. How can you maintain peace in your home?

_____

_____

_____

_____

_____

CHAPTER 5

THE BATTLE

Everything we have learned up to this moment has pointed to the battle and each chapter so far has been leading up to this moment. We have talked about preparing yourself, about linking arms with an army around you, and about doing what you can to make peace in your home and life. But now it is time for the fight, time to battle. What do you do?

If you think about a foot race, there is a moment when someone yells, "On your mark, get set, go." Using that as a framework, let's talk about what you actually do in the battle.

First, on your mark. When a runner gets ready to race, someone will yell, "On your mark."

This is the moment when the runner gets focused, gets into position for the race ahead, and preps their minds for what is to come. You have to mentally prepare for what is about to go down, for this battle. We know the enemy is ready. He has been prepping. He has a strategy on how to attack you, so we have to make sure that mentally, we are ready. Before you lunge into battle, you need to be sure you get your mind right.

The US Army created a program called Battlemind for soldiers going to and coming from a deployment. Michael Rinehart, with the Walter Reed Army Institute of Research had this to say about the initiation of that program.

> "We can't keep sending bodies where we haven't prepared their minds to go."

As I was researching this, I read that, when sending soldiers into battle, you were sending them into situations where they would see things that are not normal, be in stressful situations that many of us would never be in, and have to mentally process some of the worst situations you can be in. And again, when a soldier transitions from soldiering to civilian life, you have to be mentally prepared for that. You don't operate in civilian life like you do in a war zone. So going into a war zone and coming out of one, you need to make sure your mind is able to process that situation. That is the purpose of this military program.

My point is that you have to be sure you have prepared for what is coming mentally so that you have the opportunity to remove thoughts that are going to inhibit your ability to battle effectively. You have to remove negative thoughts, for instance, of the outcome, or emotions like fear and unbelief, and even your expectations of the result. There were certain times when Jesus couldn't heal because of the peoples' lack of faith. Yet many times we see people being healed as a result of faith. They were recipients of healing, having already had a positive outcome in their minds. "This is Jesus. I have seen him heal others. He can heal me." If you launch into a battle with this mindset that you are probably going to lose, then you probably will! "I'll pray, but my prayers are hitting the ceiling, so I am not expecting much."

This is what I mean by getting your mind right. 2 Corinthians 10:3-5

> "For though we walk in the flesh, we are not waging war according to the flesh. For the weapons of our warfare are not of the flesh

84

but have divine power to destroy strongholds. We destroy arguments and every lofty opinion raised against the knowledge of God, and take every thought captive to obey Christ."

We have to take every single thought that we have as we go into this battle captive to Christ. The enemy is going to try to make you doubt. He will come at you full force to try and make you afraid, like that roaring lion the Bible tells us about in 1 Peter 5:8. Take those thoughts captive.

But what does that mean? It is one of those churchy phrases like, "hedge of protection." What is that? Am I to walk around with a bush ringed around me? No. When we take a thought captive, it means two things. First, like we've talked before, it is responding to a thought with the truth of what God's Word says, and then it is responding with the positive of the negative thought you are having. So, scripture is important. It is the Sword of the Spirit which is what stops the attack, but also responding with some positivity can really help take a thought captive. For instance, a thought might come that you are in this all by yourself. The Word says that Jesus will never leave us nor forsake us (Hebrews 13:5). The positive thought would be recognizing that Jesus has never abandoned you before, and he has no reason to start that now. That is how you take a thought captive.

Captain Curtis Brooker, commander of Company A, 2nd Battalion, 13th Infantry Regiment said this about preparing soldiers mentally for war:

> "I think we do really good job of preparing Soldiers physically and tactically for combat. While we test them mentally through the rigors of Basic Combat Training, I'm not sure we completely prepare them for all the stressors they will face in combat."

The reason I bring this up is because you are not now, nor can you be, prepared for everything you will see in the battle. The enemy will adjust his tactics in mid-fight and sling something you haven't prepared for. You might be facing a battle at your job, dealing with a stressful issue, and so the enemy, in the midst of the battle while he is charging you head on, might send a flank to route you from behind with a sexually immoral thought, and you find yourself fighting on two fronts now. The enemy has adjusted the strategy mid-stream. Your faith and endurance will be tested, but we have to remember two very important things in this moment: First, while we have a responsibility to step up and battle, we can't forget God's promise that he would fight for us. Exodus 14:14 relays a promise to us that,

"The Lord will fight for you, and you shall hold your peace."

And secondly, that our primary role is to seek God's kingdom first, keeping our eyes on Jesus. Isaiah 26:3 promises,

"You keep him in perfect peace whose mind is stayed on you, because he trusts in you."

One of the best ways to spot the enemy's attacks is by staying close to Jesus. I've found when I am not focusing on Jesus, that's when I miss the warning signs of the attack. It is interesting that both of these verses above reference peace in the midst of the battle. When we are in the battle and stressors come, the enemy tries to route us from the side, or throws another attack into the mix, we have to realize that we can have peace in the midst of a battle

> **ONE OF THE BEST WAYS TO SPOT THE ENEMY'S ATTACK IS BY STAYING CLOSE TO JESUS.**

when Jesus remains our focus. Don't be tempted into fixing your gaze and attention on the battle. Keep focused on Jesus as he fights with you and for you.

The second part is to get set. This is the part of the race where the runner gets into the block, ready to lunge forward into the lane. Just like he runner has prepared his mind for the race, he has also prepared his equipment for the purpose of winning. Scientifically engineered shoes and clothes help him have the advantage to win. The same goes for NASCAR or the Tour de France, or any racing other sport. We even see military equipment change over time to specifically address the battle they faced. You need to do this as well spiritually, which is why the first thing you need before you step into battle is something the Word of God tells us to put on every day, the Armor of God.

Ephesians 6:10-18 tells us,

"Finally, be strong in the Lord and in the strength of his might. Put on the whole armor of God, that you may be able to stand against the schemes of the devil. For we do not wrestle against flesh and blood, but against the rulers, against the authorities, against the cosmic powers over this present darkness, against the spiritual forces of evil in the heavenly places. Therefore take up the whole armor of God, that you may be able to withstand in the evil day, and having done all, to stand firm. Stand therefore, having fastened on the belt of truth, and having put on the breastplate of righteousness, and, as shoes for your feet, having put on the readiness given by the gospel of peace. In all circumstances take up the shield of faith, with which you can extinguish all the flaming darts of the evil one; and take the helmet of salvation, and the sword of the Spirit, which is the word of God, praying at all times in the Spirit, with all prayer and supplication."

The Bible tells us in Galatians 3:27,

"For all of you who were baptized into Christ have clothed yourselves with Christ." NASB

Clothed with Christ is an interesting concept. When you put on your shirt, it covers your body. In the same way, when we put on Christ, he covers us, and he does this through the Armor of God. He asks us to put this on every day. I can remember as a kid when my mom drove us to school and work, she would always have me put on the Armor of God to prepare me for the day. It is important, and here is why:

Take the Helmet of Salvation. Acts 4:12 tells us that by the name of Jesus, there is:

"No other name by which we are saved"

Jesus is our salvation. Our salvation is found in him, so whenever you put on this helmet, you are clothing your head in Christ, your salvation. That means that you thoughts can come from a regenerated mindset because Jesus has saved you, changed you, and all of the sudden, everything is now new and the old has passed away. That means your thoughts, too, and even the sin that was formulated in your mind before you ever met Jesus, even the old sins that the enemy taunts you with. That is over and done and you have new thoughts now, all because of the fact that Jesus is your salvation. Your head is clothed in salvation.

Or the Breastplate of Righteousness. 2 Corinthians 5:21 tells us that

"We are the righteousness of God through Christ Jesus."

What is inside of your breast? Your heart, lungs, vital organs. Consider the things that give you life and keep you alive, namely, your heart pumping blood and your lungs taking in oxygen. See, we have life now because of what Jesus did for us. His death made us whole and restored to God through his righteousness. We were dead before Jesus, and because of what he did for us, we step into his righteousness, and now we are alive. This is why our breast needs to be clothed in Christ our righteousness. It is because without him, we simply are not alive!

Then we have our loins gird about with truth. John 14:6 says,

"Jesus is the way, the truth, and the life."

What happens from our loins? We reproduce. When we have our loins gird about with truth, it gives us the opportunity to reproduce that truth in our lives and in our families.

We are to have our feet shod with the preparation of the Gospel of peace. Ephesians 2:14 tells us,

"Jesus is our peace."

This means that wherever we walk, even if it is into tense situations, even in the most stressful moments, we walk in and peace is there because our feet are covered in Jesus Christ, the former Prince of Peace who is now King of Kings and the King of Peace!

We have the Sword of the Spirit which is the Word of God. John 1 reminds us that He is the Word of God that became flesh and dwelt among us. Jesus Christ is the Word of God, the Sword of the Spirit, and lastly, the Shield of Faith. Hebrews 12:2 tells us,

"Looking to Jesus, the author and perfecter of our faith."

Your faith started with Jesus and it will be perfected in Jesus. So what this means is that when you put on the armor of God, you are literally clothing yourself in Jesus Christ. I love the idea of a force field in sci-fi movies, when the ship or the city is protected by this invisible deterrent that stops the enemy's attack. When you put on the Armor of God and you are clothing yourself in Christ. It is like you are walking into the battle with a force field. I wish that we could see with our natural eyes into the spirit realm simply because I would love to see how many arrows and attacks that come against us that Jesus repels without us ever knowing about it. That is a mind-boggling concept to me. How many attacks do I never face because he is protecting me? I firmly believe that God allows situations to come into our lives to grow us or build us or remove things that are detrimental to our purpose, so that is why we experience these attacks, yet still, I know that Jesus is blocking way more than he is allowing! How incredible is it that the very armor that God gives us is the person of Jesus Christ, who has already won the victory!

We have to battle from this mindset, that even when the enemy changes tactics, or throws something at us we don't expect, when we are clothed in Christ by his armor, we can not only withstand, but repel the attack of the enemy. We can have confidence in his victory! We can overcome because Jesus has.

That is the second part of get set, and that is the confidence we have in Jesus. Proverbs 3:26 and Psalm 27:1-3 tells us,

> "For the Lord will be your confidence and will keep your foot from being caught."

> "The Lord is my light and my salvation; whom shall I fear? The Lord is the stronghold of my life; of whom shall I be afraid? When evildoers assail me to eat up my flesh, my adversaries and foes, it is they who stumble and fall. Though an army encamp against me, my heart shall not fear; though war arise against me, yet I will be confident."

How many times has it felt like the enemy has his army encamped around you, and all they are there to do is to eat your flesh? It can feel like that when we are struggling with work issues, or there are problems in your family. We have all experienced situations like this, where we feel like that army is waiting right there to destroy us, but the Bible is super clear, that we are not confident in ourselves or our ability to save, but we are confident in Jesus Christ and the victory that he brings into our lives.

There's a song out lately that has really encouraged me. It is called "Confident," which says, "I'm confident your faithfulness will see me through." You might need to hear this right now, that you are going to get through whatever battle you are facing. You are going to be okay once the dust settles. You have Jesus with you. I realize you can't control everything in the battle, and you aren't going to be prepared for every arrow, but be confident, because at the end of the day, God's faithfulness will see you through. Trust him!

And lastly, get ready, get set, go. It is go time. The battle begins. What do you do?

Every battle, no matter the size of it, nor the speed at which it approached, begins with prayer. That is what I did when we got the bad report with my daughter, and that is what we should always do! Some of that prayer needs to be directed at God. You need to ask for his faithfulness, his intervention, his protection. You ask him to stand by his Word and remind him of his Word and faithfulness, and call out to him for help in the time of trouble.

And listen, don't, even for a second, be afraid to remind God of what he's promised both to you personally and in Scripture. Look, God is smart and he can remember what he said. Truthfully, he doesn't need reminding. But we need to do this for two reasons: we need to hear it, to remind ourselves as we remind him, and secondly, because the enemy needs to hear you remind him of what God has said and that you are still standing on that promise. The enemy needs to hear it. In every situation, when the arrows are flying towards you, you need to turn to prayer first and you need to remind you and the enemy that this is what God has said, and that no matter what, I am going to trust in God. I am going to be confident, even when I feel like the enemy is encamped around me.

Also, some of our prayer needs to be directed towards the enemy. I don't mean praying to him. That would not be good! But here's what you do, you tell him the truth. Tell him of God's promises and faithfulness. "God has delivered me before, and Satan, I am remind you that since he has done it before, he can do it again. I am going to trust in him." You rebuke and resist him. James 4:7 promises us,

> "Resist the devil, and he will flee from you."

One of the biggest reasons that men and homes are being attacked right now is simply because men are not standing up and resisting the enemy! It is a promise that if we resist, the enemy will flee. "Well, I keep falling into temptation." Resist! The reason you are falling into temptation is because you are not doing what the Word says, which is just to resist him Notice, it doesn't say defeat him, or wound him. No, all you have to do is resist him. God promises us a way of escape (1 Corinthians 10:13), but I believe that way doesn't reveal itself until we resist.

Continuing on, you remind him who has already won. You demand he stop coming against you and your family, and you cancel his assignments and schemes. God has given us power over the works of the enemy (Luke 10:19). This is a promise! So we have to step up in these moments when the battle comes and remind Satan that we have authority over him and power to overcome him through Jesus Christ. We have to put him in his place, but all in the name of Jesus. You need to be careful not to tell the enemy what to do if you don't know the person behind the name you are throwing out. The sons of Sceva found this out the hard way in Acts 19. You need to be sure before you launch into spiritual warfare that you are completely in God's camp, and not expecting a half-hearted relation-ship with Jesus to be the thing that helps you win the day.

Some prayer is directed at God, some at the enemy, and we need to be sure we pray in the Spirit and in the understanding. Paul encourages us to do this in 1 Corinthians 14. Some of that prayer is going to be in En-glish, but some needs to be in the Spirit. Why? Sometimes you need to stop speaking and allow the Holy Spirit to pray what he wants to pray, to allow the deep in God to call out to the deep in you. This is God warring for you in prayer.

That is why some of my prayer in the shower that night was in the Spirit and some in English. I find that when I allow the Holy Spirit to intercede for me in that moment, that he build me up, encourages me, strengthens me, empowers me, and all of the sudden, the battling I am doing in English is much more productive and overcoming.

As a very important side note, since we are talking about praying in the Spirit, is that you need to be sure that you understand salvation, baptism, and baptism in the Holy Spirit, and that you have engaged in each. God has three main steps for every human being that has ever lived, or will ever. First, is salvation. Romans 10:9 says,

> "If you confess with your mouth that Jesus is Lord and believe in your heart that God raised him from the dead, you will be saved."

Salvation is the restoration of the relationship we originally had with God, and without it, you neither have God in your camp, nor do you have the victor going to battle with and for you. Second is baptism. Acts 22:16 tells us,

> "And now why do you wait? Rise and be baptized and wash away your sins, calling on his name."

Baptism is not just a quick dip in a giant bathtub. When we say yes to Jesus and are saved, we are crucified with Christ (Galatians 2:20), and that means we die to our old nature with Jesus on the Cross. Death means a dead body, and something has to be done with a dead body. With Jesus, they buried him in a grave in the form of a cave in a garden. For us, we bury our old nature in a watery grave in the form of baptism via immersion. Jesus was raised on the third day, and likewise, we are raised in that moment to walk in the new life we find in Jesus. There is a supernatural transaction that takes place in that moment where, just like it says in 2 Corinthians 5:17,

> "Therefore, if anyone is in Christ, he is a new creation. The old has passed away; behold, the new has come."

Our old nature is dead, buried, and no longer has any control over us. And lastly is the infilling of the Holy Spirit. Acts 2:38-39 says,

> "Repent and be baptized every one of you in the name of Jesus Christ for the forgiveness of your sins, and you will receive the gift of the Holy Spirit. For the promise is for you and for your children and for all who are far off, everyone whom the Lord our God calls to himself."

This is the power of God, the very power that raised Christ from the dead, as we see in Romans 8:11,

> "The Spirit of God, who raised Jesus from the dead, lives in you. And just as God raised Christ Jesus from the dead, he will give life to your mortal bodies by this same Spirit living within you."

I ask God every single day for God to fill me fresh and new with the Holy Spirit. I need a new infilling every day! This is not hard to do. It doesn't take going down to the altar and having a team pray over you for an hour. Of course not! If salvation is done by confessing Jesus as Lord, and baptism is as easy as being immersed in water, then being filled with the Holy Spirit is that easy, too. Why would God make something he wants you to have so difficult to get? Luke 11:13 promises us,

> "If you (fathers) then, who are evil, know how to give good gifts to your children, how much more will the heavenly Father give the Holy Spirit to those who ask him!"

Just ask him for his Holy Spirit, and you will receive him! And the why is just as important. We see this in 2 Peter 1:3,

"By his divine power (the Holy Spirit), God has given us everything we need for living a godly life."

If you want to battle and win, you need to be saved, baptized, and filled with the Holy Spirit.

So the first part of the actual battle is prayer, and just as important is the second part, scripture. You need to speak the Word of God in the battle for several reasons.

First, it is what sustains you. Matthew 4:4 says,

"But he (Jesus) answered, 'It is written, 'Man shall not live by bread alone, but by every word that comes from the mouth of God.''"

Every word that comes from God's mouth is bread and sustenance for you, so you need it to sustain you in the midst of a tough battle. There will be times when you want to give up. The battle probably won't be a 30 minute prayer session and that is it. It is probably going to be an ongoing thing that drags out over some time. You will need something to sustain you in that process. That is why you need to ingest the Word of God. Many times I see battles where God is trying to work something out of me, and that can be tough.

YOU NEED TO REMIND YOURSELF OF GOD'S WORD WHEN YOU CAN'T SEE THE PROMISE COMING TO PASS.

I know, in those moments, I need something to sustain me in the midst of the battle. I need to remind myself of his Word in those moments when I can't see those promises coming to pass. God's Word is what does this.

Second, it is the truth when the enemy is shooting lies at you. Proverbs 30:5-6 tells us,

> "Every word of God proves true; he is a shield to those who take refuge in him."

His truth is s shield for us, so when the enemy is speaking those lies to us, when we are tired or stressed, when we are laying in out beds at night and the enemy attacks us with lies, we can lean into God's Word and refute those lies with truth. "You are never going to solve that situation at work." "You are never going to get out of that financial hole." "Your spouse is never going to be enough for you." Lies, lies, lies.

Third, God's Word, scripture, accomplishes that for which it was sent. Isaiah 55:11 says,

> "So shall my word be that goes out from my mouth; it shall not re-turn to me empty, but it shall accomplish that which I purpose, and shall succeed in the thing for which I sent it."

Does this mean that if God said something then it is going to instantly happen and come to pass, that if I need healing that God is going to in-stantly heal me? No, of course not. We don't always know why God does what he does, nor do we understand the plan he has for us all the time, but if God has spoken a word or a promise, it will come to pass. We have to be super careful in these moments not to create false expectations of how God's Word will be accomplished. Neither you nor I are God, and as a result, we cannot expect God to do something specifically how we want it. Our job is to trust.

The Bible is not only the Sword you wield in the fight, but it is also the battle plan written out. There is a saying that "The Army plans. A Marine improvises." Which do you find yourself doing more in the midst of the battle? Following the plan, or improvising? I find that, many times, I go nto the battle with no plan, only improvising along the way. It can leave me exposed, at times. This is not smart! God has given us the battle plan n his Word, and while there are benefits to both planning and improvising n isolation, it is important that we follow the battle plan and be ready to mprovise as well.

Fourth, it builds your faith. Romans 10:17 says,

> "Faith comes by hearing, and hearing through the word of Christ."

You should read your Bible out loud as often as you can. I often do the Bible in a year plan, and I do like to read it so I can jot down notes and highlight verses, but I always feel more encouraged and always feel like have bigger faith when I turn on the "read out loud" feature while I am getting ready for work. There is something about hearing the Word of God spoken in my ears. It is all about Romans 10:17. I am hearing the Word and my faith is growing.

Fifth, it is what defeats the darkness. Psalm 119:105 tells us,

> "Your word is a lamp unto my feet and a light unto my path."

John 1:5 says,

> "The light (Jesus) shines in the darkness, and the darkness has not overcome it."

f you have darkness in your world right now, the only thing that is going to change that is the Word of God, the light. You may have darkness in your ife, but if you will allow God access to everything by making him Lord of everything in your life, you will find that, not only will the light shine, the darkness will be overcome.

So we've had prayer, scripture, and now the third part of "go," worship.

A mighty weapon in your hand is actually one that is in your mouth too! Isaiah 30:29-32 tells us,

"But the people of God will sing a song of joy, like the songs at the holy festivals. You will be filled with joy, as when a flutist leads a group of pilgrims to Jerusalem, the mountain of the Lord—to the Rock of Israel. And the Lord will make his majestic voice heard. He will display the strength of his mighty arm. It will descend with devouring flames, with cloudbursts, thunderstorms, and huge hailstones. At the Lord's command, the Assyrians will be shattered. He will strike them down with his royal scepter. And as the Lord strikes them with his rod of punishment, his people will celebrate with tambourines and harps. Lifting his mighty arm, he will fight the Assyrians." NLT

Imagine this: God and his army rushing down the mountainside to slay the army of the enemy, all the while he is riding into battle, not on horses and chariots, but upon the praise and worship of his people. What an incredible thought, but it is more than that. Worship is a powerful way to fight the enemy, as it puts God in the proper place in your life, allowing him to unleash "the strength of his might arm" on your behalf.

Be sure you don't forget to worship God in the battle, not just before or after. Look, Satan has his secret weapons, but we do too, and worship is one of them! Remember Paul and Silas in prison. It wasn't might and strength that broke the chains. It was worship! Worship has immense power to overcome the enemy, so don't forget to do it.

Lastly, the fourth part of "go" is use your army. We have talked about this a lot, but it is that important. You need your army. You may have a battle like I did that night I went to war with the enemy for my daughter, and you are going to have moments like this when you get an intense burden to pray, to war. You will hear the battle cry in your spirit and jump into action. But often, the war isn't won in a day, and you will need people around you praying, warring, lifting you up, going to bat for you. If you are facing a battle right now, don't try to be the hero and go it alone. Tell your team. Let them fight with you. Be sure that you are shooting a text to your top three to let them know what is going on and to gear up for the fight.

So how do you battle? It takes lots of prayer, and not the "God I hope it works out" kind of prayer. It takes intense, honest, vigilant, that aggressive against the enemy kind of prayer from a place of confidence in God and victory through Jesus. Don't pray, "Lord if it be your will." That may seem wrong to you, but that kind of prayer isn't a faith prayer, it is a doubt prayer, because it leaves an excuse for when the outcome isn't what you expect. Pray from a place of confidence knowing that God can be trusted.

It is going to take lots of Scripture. Nothing defeats the enemy like God's Word. David used it. Jesus used it. Jesus WAS the Word and he still used the Word! It is like Jesus pulled off his arm and started whooping the devil with it! I know that seems silly, but if the Word that became flesh used the Word to fight, we need to as well. Speak the Word of God over your situation. Speak the Word of God over your family, not just in prayer, but in random moments throughout the day, too. One time my wife had to take a trip to Washington DC, and after a long day of travel with a layover and shuttles and chaos in busy airports, she finally got settled in. She messaged me that she was finally there but that she was exhausted. I texted back that she should go to sleep and get some rest. She responded with, "There is no rest for the weary." So I sent back a text, honestly, half kidding and half serious. It said,

> "Come to me, all who labor and are heavy laden, and I will give you rest. Take my yoke upon you, and learn from me, for I am gentle and lowly in heart, and you will find rest for your souls. For my yoke is easy, and my burden is light." (Matthew 11:28-30)

She didn't respond that night, but I have since learned that she just went to sleep, however, I know she read the text. Now, while I was partially joking, trying to "Jesus Juke" her, she did read the Word of God, and specifically, a verse that addressed her very immediate situation. We need to be doing this every day with our families. I don't mean going nuts by only responding to every word uttered at your house with a Bible verse (you are probably going to get hit!), but we need to be speaking the life found in the Word of God over our families on a daily basis.

It is going to take lots of worship. Make sure you worship and do it often. Let your kids hear you worship. You don't have to be a vocalist, but you have to vocalize it. You don't have to walk down the hall singing the latest worship song, but it will change the atmosphere of your home if you family hears you declaring to the Lord that he is good and that you love him, that he is worthy of praise and that you owe everything to him. If you want worship to be present in your home, then you are the one who needs to make that happen, and by example.

> **WORSHIP. YOU DON'T HAVE TO BE A VOCALIST BUT YOU DO HAVE TO VOCALIZE IT.**

It is going to take lots of teamwork. You will go faster alone, but further together. You will lose alone, but you will win together.

In the heat of the battle, you need to be prepared for moments of extreme victory. Be prepared for moments when you feel utterly defeated. But keep trusting God, keep believing his Word, keep digging in, in terms of faith, refusing to give up or give in.

Be prepared for God to speak to you as well. Sometimes, it is in the heat of the battle that God speaks the most clearly. When our senior pastor at a church where I served lost his daughter in a car wreck, he drove up on the wreck, and rather than questioning God in that moment, it was in the heat of that moment that God gave him the dream for a ministry that ended up leading thousands of young adults to Jesus. In the middle of the worst battle of your life, God can speak to you the very word that will change your life forever. Be prepared for that!

Be prepared for the battle not to go the way you expect it to go. Don't put those expectations out there so that the enemy can use them to challenge your faith in God. Your family member may not get healed. Your relationship with you spouse may not be mended. Your kid mid twist off anyway. As long as it is up to you, live at peace." Some things are out of your control, but whether God does what you want or not, do you still trust him? Is he still your God? Are you going to stay faithful even if the outcome isn't what you expect? Sometimes the only thing you can control in life is yourself. Even if it doesn't end how you wanted, he is still God and knows what is best! Fight hard, and trust him no matter the outcome.

The battle you are facing will not last forever, it will not overcome you, and you will not lose, as long as you keep the main thing the main thing, and that is Jesus as Lord, as your protector, as your champion, as your leader, and if you operate under the power of the Holy Spirit, who gives you everything you need to win against what you are facing. That battle belongs to the Lord, and by his power, you are already victorious!

Small Group Questions

1. How important is the mental preparation before a battle?

_____

_____

_____

_____

_____

2. What role does your positive or negative thinking have in the outcome of the battle?

_____

_____

_____

_____

_____

3. How do you typically respond to unexpected attacks in your life or family?

_____

_____

_____

_____

_____

4. What does it look like to have peace in the midst of a battle?

_____

_____

_____

_____

_____

5. How important is the Armor of God in your daily life, in battle or peace-time?

_____

_____

_____

_____

_____

6. Is there a piece of armor that you connect with the most? Why?

_____

_____

_____

_____

_____

7. Why is confidence (in God, in yourself, in the promise) so important in the battle?

_____

_____

_____

_____

_____

8. Why does reminding God of his promise help in the battle?

_____

_____

_____

_____

_____

9. What does it look like to be aggressive towards the enemy in prayer?

_____

_____

10. Why is scripture so effective in the fight?

_____

_____

_____

_____

_____

11. What role does worship play in the battle? Is it an effective weapon? Why/why not?

_____

_____

_____

_____

_____

12. How do you deal with the outcome when it is not what you expected?

_____

_____

_____

_____

_____

CHAPTER 6

THE AFTERMATH

don't know if you have ever taken the time to look on the back of a shampoo bottle, but there is always a phrase, or some form of this phrase, that is both super informational, and partially scary, because it makes you question the overall intelligence of the population. The phrase is this:

Lather. Rinse. Repeat.

We're in bad trouble if we have to tell people who can read how to use shampoo! Nevertheless, these are instructions on what to do if you want to get your hair clean. We can use this same pattern as a template for what we do once the battle is over. I would suggest you even do this once you have finished the little skirmishes that happen from time to time, but rather than lather, rinse, repeat, let's adjust the wording a little to:

Learn. Praise. Repeat.

So let's spend this last chapter talking about those three things and how they can help you as you battle against the enemy for yourself, your marriage, and your family.

First, learn. You never stop learning, and the moment you do, then you are about to get clobbered. In terms of the battle, one of the most important things you can do is to learn from what you just went through. Roman statesman Cicero said,

> "To be ignorant of what occurred before you were born is to remain always a child."

There is quotation from a movie, one I referenced before, Thirteen Days, where John F. Kennedy's character mentions a book called the Guns of August. JFK really did read this book, and many credit his takeaway from that book as being a huge part of what kept us from spiraling into nuclear war. While the quote is not 100% historical, the idea from the book is, and the lesson definitely is. So here is what the character quoted:

> You know, last summer I read a book, The Guns of August. I wish every man on that blockade line had read that book. It's World War One; there's thirteen million killed; it was all because the militaries of both alliances believed they were so highly attuned to one another's movements and dispositions, they could predict one another's intentions, but all their theories were based on the last war. And the world and technology had changed, and those lessons were no longer valid, but it was all they knew, so the orders went out, couldn't be rescinded. And your man in the field, his family at home, they couldn't even tell you the reasons why their lives were being destroyed.

Imagine being a soldier and having to face a new battle, but still using the same tactics and making the same mistakes as the last war? It would be devastating. Much like this analogy, we find ourselves at a clear disadvantage when we look back on what we just marched through and learn nothing.

Every skirmish, every battle, has a lesson to teach you. Sometimes those essons are about yourself. Sometimes those lessons are about how to espond, or about the people around you. Perhaps even your tactics and modes of operation. No matter the lesson, there is always something you can learn from your previous battle.

Think back on your last battle. Did you learn anything from it? Did God show you anything? Did you notice things about yourself that needed to be addressed or adjusted for the next battle? And honestly, the things you learn are not always negatives that need addressing. You might look back on a battle where God miraculously intervened and be moved to praise him in this moment. It builds your faith and trust in God for the next fight!

Be sure to take time to connect with guys in your life as well. You would be surprised what you would learn about your own life and battles by studying others and their battles. If you will be hungry enough to learn and grow, you can actually be better prepared for your next fight by learning from battles you were never in to begin with! When a buddy comes out of a battle, take time to connect with him. Ask him to tell you what he learned, what he could/would do differently, what he did well. You will find that you are better prepared and more equipped to win the next battle.

One of the bad things about not learning from your previous engagements is the repetition of the same types of battles God might allow you to face. That means if you don't learn from the battle, God may allow another similar battle to try to teach you the lesson again. And again. And again. You get the picture.

One time I was praying and I felt like I was in a season where I was going in circles, much like you might feel by being in this cycle of battle. In my time praying, God showed me the 610 loop in Houston, Texas. This is a super busy roadway makes an entire circle around the city, has tons of traffic, and tons of entrances and exits. I watched from above as the cars flew past, and I found myself focusing on one vehicle. I knew God was showing me that it was me and that I was on a loop in my life. I knew God had an exit for me. I knew he wanted me to go somewhere and do something great, but I was simply driving around Houston in what seemed to be an endless loop. It mimicked what I was feeling in my heart and spirit. I realized in that moment that my life experiences, while not exactly the same, would repeat themselves until I realized what God was trying to show me. The battles I faced from week to week were not exactly the same, but the lesson was always similar. I just wasn't getting it! God showed me that he would keep me in a loop until I learned what I needed to learn to get to my exit, and that he would allow me to endure the traffic for another round if it meant I would finally exit. I had to learn the traffic and the flow and learn how to manage my vehicle and obey the law, and that when I was functioning the right way on the loop, I could take my exit in due time. God never keeps us on a loop to punish us or hold us back. He does it out of love to prepare us for the next thing.

| **LEARN FROM YOUR LAST BATTLE AND PRAISE GOD NO MATTER THE OUTCOME.** | My encouragement to you in this moment is to look back on your last few battles. What did you learn? What should you have learned? And as you go forward, be sure you take time to do this first step, and that is to learn. |

Second, praise. Look, it is super easy to worship God when you've won the battle. We shout hallelujah, we sing to the Lord, we tell our family and friends that the victory is won. We go nuts, and we should! It is a wonderful thing when we win! So there should be praise in your heart towards God when the outcome is favorable and peace is in your life once again. That joy and excitement in that moment is euphoric.

But what about when the outcome isn't good? What about when the result is not what you expected? What if the outcome means healing didn't happen, or the job fell through, or the teen twisted off anyway? Worship is easy in the victory, but it is in the uncertainty of a defeat or a draw, or an outcome that wasn't expected, where worship is difficult. That is because what is really God to you will surface in that moment. Here is what I mean.

There have been plenty of times when I worshiped my expected outcome more than the one who gives me victory. I've wanted the job, or expected the healing, and when those things didn't work out, I found myself angry or disappointed or broken-hearted. There's nothing like an unmet expectation to show you what you are really worshiping.

But when you can praise God even when things don't go the way you want, you know that your god is God and that your hope is in him, not in what he can do for you. Get to a place where you can confidently say, "God, this didn't end like I thought it would, but you are still God, and no matter what, I am going to trust you." I love what Job said in Job 13:15, and I hope that in every moment I can have the same faith in God when he said,

"Though he slay me, I will hope in him."

Though he slay me? Though the storm has ravaged me? Though the battle didn't go as I had planned? Of course. Let me ask you this: what other choice do we have? Listen, you do have a choice in following God. He is not going to force you to follow him, but after you have experienced the goodness of God, how could you turn anywhere else? I am reminded of that scene in the Gospel of John when many disciples turned away from Jesus. He then looked at the disciples and asked if they were going to leave, too. God help us respond like Peter did in that moment in John 6:68,

"Lord, where would we go?" TPT

The truth is, there is no other place to go. If you are a Christian, a child of God, then you have reached a place where you understand that it is in Christ "that I live and move and have my being." (Acts 17:28). My life is found in Jesus, and even though he allows storms in my life, I have no other choice but to trust him and praise him and be faithful to him. It isn't because I don't have a choice. It is because I don't want another choice. I he is everything to me and if he is where I find fulfillment, then that has to be true in the good and the bad times, sunny skies and gray, in the sweetness of victory and the pain of defeat.

I am convinced that this is why David was such a successful warrior. I am sure he had skills as a leader and as a soldier, but David wasn't the biggest guy on the field. David wasn't the most skilled warrior in the bunch. He wasn't Samson who could slay 1000 Philistines with a donkey's jawbone. But David had something that is necessary in our lives today: he was a man after God's own heart. This is not a descriptor that David gave to himself. God said that about David in both 1 Samuel 13:14 where he alludes to David and in Acts 13:22, where he outright says it was David. What does that mean, a man after God's own heart? Worship, that's what! We're talking about a man who wrote numerous songs of praise to God. And don't just think they were songs after the victories. He wrote songs of praise to God when he was running from Saul, who was trying to kill him, when he was alone in the wilderness hiding in a cave, when his son died, when he was fleeing from his son Absalom who was trying to usurp the throne. David knew a principle that we need to embrace, and that is praising God in the good and the bad, the victories and the defeats.

This is going to reveal your heart in your life. You will find out quickly what it is you have been worshiping all along. Be sure to praise God. Sing of his faithfulness. Tell him of his goodness. I definitely don't want God to slay me, but I pray I will still worship, even when it isn't going the way I thought it would.

Finally, repeat. Your life will be a steady cycle of preparation, battle, learning, praising, and repeating it all over again. That might sound bleak to you, but I hope you see the truth, and that is with every cycle, you have the opportunity to get better, to grow, to develop, to change, to hone your skills, to sharpen your faith, to live more powerfully, and to protect your house with passion and authority. Not perfection, just getting one step better. That is what your life is and that is what God is using these battles for.

I would love to tell you that there is going to be a moment in your life while you are still young and spry when all the battles end. Unfortunately, the battles end when you cross that threshold in Heaven. The good news, however, is that I find that certain battles do get easier. When I was younger, sexual immorality was a battle I had to fight often, but after God delivered me from that lifestyle, I found that, while the enemy still attacked, the battles were easier and easier

IF YOU ARE REPEATING THE SAME BATTLES, GOD IS TRYING TO TEACH YOU SOMETHING.

to win. So some relief does come in that. I have also learned that the old Pentecostal saying, "New levels, new devils" is somewhat true. I may not be facing the same battles I faced as a 20 year old, but the enemy still attacks, seemingly on a grander scale. This is a part of why it is so important to keep battle ready when things are going well.

In John 16, Jesus was telling the disciples what would happen as the time for his death drew near. In verse 33, he tells them,

"In the world you will have tribulation."

In terms of our focus here, that verse sounds like this,

"In this godless world, you are going to have battles."

Like it or not, we are going to face battles, but there is news so good that I can keep it from you no longer. Read the rest of that verse,

"But take heart; I have overcome the world."

Jesus has overcome, and if we align ourselves with Jesus Christ and his army, we will found ourselves standing beside him in victory. Troubles are going to come, but we have the ability to win this war because Jesus has already won, and we are on his side!

I encourage you to learn, praise, and repeat those two often. With every battle, get smarter. With every victory, praise him. With every struggle, grow closer to him. And even when things don't go your way, be sure you praise him. If you live a lifestyle of learn, praise, and repeat, you are going to find yourself in a place of victory.

Small Group Questions

1. Why is learning from your previous battles so important?

_____

_____

_____

_____

_____

2. What is something you learned from a previous battle that helped in a latter one?

_____

_____

_____

_____

_____

3. Is there a common thread I your battles that you think God is trying to show you? Explain.

_____

_____

_____

_____

_____

4. Why is praise such an important part of the aftermath?

_____

_____

_____

_____

_____

5. Praise is easier in victories than in defeats. Why is it so important to praise, even if it didn't go your way?

_____

_____

_____

_____

_____

6. Do you find it hard to trust God in the battle? Explain.

_____

_____

_____

_____

_____

7. Name some ways you can grow your faith and trust in God for the battle.

_____

_____

_____

_____

_____

8. Have you ever been in a bad battle and found yourself angry at God for either allowing it or not intervening as you would have liked? How did you process that?

_____

_____

_____

_____

_____

9. Do you feel like you are in a loop of similar battles right now? If so, what is God trying to teach you?

_____

_____

_____

_____

_____

10. How does the fact that "you are going to have battles" sit with you? And how does knowing Jesus has overcome the world change how you battle?

_____

_____

_____

_____

_____

CHAPTER 7

THE CHARGE

Nehemiah is an incredible little book in the latter part of the Old Testament that tells the story of a captive Jewish man and cup bearer to King Artaxerxes of Persia named Nehemiah. The mandate given to him by God was no small one. He was to return to Jerusalem and rebuild the walls of the city. He was broken-hearted upon hearing that the city had been destroyed, as the destruction was a foreshadowing of the annihilation of his nation. One would think the king would not care about Nehemiah's situation, however, the king not only felt for him, the king sent him back with a contingency of people to rebuild the walls.

As they began the work, there were some in the surrounding nations who wished to destroy them and the work they were doing. We catch up to the story in two short passages in Nehemiah 4:7-9, 13-14, which says,

> When Sanballat, Tobiah, the Arabs, the Ammonites and the people of Ashdod heard that the repairs to Jerusalem's walls had gone ahead and that the gaps were being closed, they were very angry. They all plotted together to come and fight against Jerusalem and stir up trouble against it. But we prayed to our God and posted a guard day and night to meet this threat.

Therefore I stationed some of the people behind the lowest points of the wall at the exposed places, posting them by families, with their swords, spears and bows. After I looked things over, I stood up and said to the nobles, the officials and the rest of the people "Don't be afraid of them. Remember the Lord, who is great and awesome, and fight for your families, your sons and your daughters, your wives and your homes."

I know there are times when you have felt like the world is crashing in on you, the stress is high, the tension is on, and all you are doing is trying to rebuild what God told you to rebuild, all the while people and nations are plotting your destruction. I get it. I have felt like that, too, at times. You are working hard, doing the right thing, trying your hardest to honor God, to lead your family well, and the enemy is out there beyond the walls planning another battle. Sometimes it can get overwhelming. Sometimes, you can be like those men with Nehemiah rebuilding the walls of Jerusalem, afraid and worried about the looming attack. Again, I get it.

> **YOU NEED JESUS. YOU NEED THE HOLY SPIRIT. YOU NEED A TEAM. NEVER BATTLE ALONE.**

But let me take a moment here at the end, as we recap what we've talked about in these pages, to remind you to stand firm. Be the man. Stand and fight against the enemy. Resist him. See, the men and nations may have prepared themselves for battle against Nehemiah and his men, however, the Bible tells us that God thwarted their attack, frustrating the plot, and bringing victory to Nehemiah. That, however, is what happened after he challenged them to stand firm, to not be afraid, to fight for their families and homes.

You need to prepare yourself for the battle. You need to make Jesus Lord of your life. You need to be baptized. You need to be filled with the Holy Spirit. You need a team around you and a church family to stand by your side. You need to war in prayer and in the Word and in worship. You need to earn and praise God and repeat it all over again, but none of this happens unless you take your position, put on your armor, stand between the enemy and your family, link arms with your brothers to the right and left, trust God, have faith, and get ready to fight.

You are going to have to address issues in your life. Things like your perspective, any idolatry hidden deep within, your expectations, your attitude, your anger and pride, and more. You are going to have to address issues in your marriage. Things like your intimacy, both sexual and asexual, your communication, your finances, your devotion to God and each other. You are going to have to address issues in your family. Things like rebellion and isolation, frustration and fear and abandonment. To address these issues, it takes a man willing to take the blows, take the hits, swallow pride, be the first to seek peace, the first to deal with a situation, yet all in love and concern and the deepest desire to bring righteousness and honor and the love of God into your home. Some issues are going to be a breeze to deal with, yet others, you are going to have to fight like there is no tomorrow, tooth and nail. Those fights will be bloody and hard, but you are going to win. Hear me man of God. You can will and you will win as long as you focus on Jesus in the process.

So as a final challenge, let me mimic the words of Nehemiah to you in this moment to encourage you in the midst of the battle:

Do not be afraid. Remember the Lord your God,
who is great and awesome (and victorious!).
Fight for yourself. Fight for your marriage. Fight for your family.
Because of Jesus Christ, your victorious and conquering King,
you have already won the BATTLE!

BATTLE

NOTES

OTHER TITLES BY

JASON JOHN COWART

FREE - Winning the War Against Sexual Immorality

21 DAYS - To Kickstart Your Prayer Life

5 THINGS - 5 Things Parents Can Do to Help Their
Teens Overcome

Coming Soon

Surviving The Wilderness

Walk Around Grace

Titles are available at

www.jasonjohncowart.com

or at www.amazon.com

Made in the USA
Columbia, SC
13 May 2022

60335135R00086